VIOLENT FIRST CONTACT IN VENEZUELA

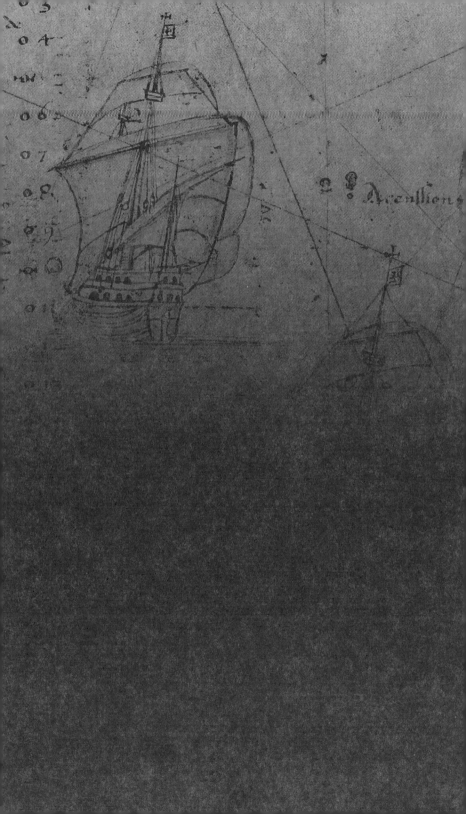

VIOLENT FIRST CONTACT IN VENEZUELA

Nikolaus Federmann's *Indian History*

Peter Hess

The Pennsylvania State University Press
University Park, Pennsylvania

Frontispiece Detail from Diogo Ribeiro, *Welser Map* (fragment), Seville, 1530. Studienbibliothek Dillingen, Mapp. 1.

Library of Congress Cataloging-in-Publication Data

Names: Federmann, Nikolaus, active 16th century, author. | Hess, Peter Andreas, translator, writer of introduction.
Title: Violent first contact in Venezuela : Nikolaus Federmann's Indian history / [translated by] Peter Hess.
Other titles: Indianische historia. English | Latin American originals ; 18.
Description: University Park, Pennsylvania : The Pennsylvania State University Press, [2021] | Series: Latin American originals ; 18 | Includes bibliographical references and index.
Summary: "The first English translation of Jndianische Historia, an account by the German mercenary Nikolaus Federmann of the incursion he led to the interior of Venezuela in 1530–31. Includes a critical introduction that contextualizes Federmann's firsthand account within the broader Spanish colonial system"—Provided by publisher.
Identifiers: LCCN 2021027723 | ISBN 9780271091792 (paperback)
Subjects: LCSH: Indians of South America—Venezuela. | Venezuela—History—To 1556. | America—Early accounts to 1600.
Classification: LCC E125.F3 F2813 2021 | DDC 987/.01—dc23
LC record available at https://lccn.loc.gov/2021027723

The Pennsylvania State University Press is a member of the Association of University Presses.

It is the policy of The Pennsylvania State University Press to use acid-free paper. Publications on uncoated stock satisfy the minimum requirements of American National Standard for Information Sciences—Permanence of Paper for Printed Library Material, ANSI z39.48–1992.

CONTENTS

Acknowledgments / vii
Foreword / ix
Map / xiii

Introduction / 1

Indian History / 23
    To the noble and mighty Johann Wilhelm von Laubenberg / 23
    [Chapter 1] About the departure of Nikolaus Federmann the Younger from Spain / 24
    [Chapter 2] How Nikolaus Federmann acted after his arrival in Coro / 35
    [Chapter 3] The beginning of Nikolaus Federmann's journey from Coro inland / 37
    [Chapter 4] The Nation of the Jirajaras / 37
    [Chapter 5] The Nation of the Ayamanes / 39
    [Chapter 6] The Nation of the Gayones / 49
    [Chapter 7] The Nation of the Achagua / 52
    [Chapter 8] The Nation of the Caquetíos / 56
    [Chapter 9] The Nation of the Cuibas / 62
    [Chapter 10] The Nation of the Coyones / 73
    [Chapter 11] The Nation of the Guaiqueríes / 77
    [Chapter 12] The Nation of the Caquetíos / 90
    [Chapter 13] The Nation of the Ciparicotos / 96
    [Chapter 14] Return from the back country to Coro / 102
    [Chapter 15] Return to Spain from Coro / 103
    [Chapter 16] Return to Augsburg from Spain / 106

Selected Bibliography / 109
Index / 113

ACKNOWLEDGMENTS

This book would not have become a reality without the encouragement of many colleagues who promised me that they would use
my translation of Federmann's *Indian History* in their classes. I had
pondered this project for almost a decade, and the opportunity arose
when the College of Liberal Arts at the University of Texas at Austin,
under Dean Randy Diehl and Senior Associate Dean Richard Flores,
granted me release time in 2018, at the end of my second term as
department chair. I am grateful for their support. I am also indebted
to Michael Shensky, Geographic Information System (GIS) and
Geospatial Data Coordinator at the University of Texas Libraries, for
creating the map for this volume.

The Herzog August Bibliothek Wolfenbüttel has been my scholarly home away from home for a number of years. The library
provides an ideal research environment, supported by a wonderful
professional staff and enriched by an ingenious community of guest
scholars. The library owns the first edition of Federmann's text,
which I worked with on a daily basis, as well as every imaginable
dictionary and lexicon necessary for this kind of painstaking detective
work. I was delighted that the Herzog August Bibliothek provided
me with a five-month research grant in summer and fall 2018 to
cover travel and living expenses in Wolfenbüttel. I wish to thank the
library, Director Peter Burschel, and the state of Niedersachsen for
this generous support that enabled me to translate the text and write
the introduction.

I also want to express my gratitude to Matthew Restall and the
editorial board for including my translation in Latin American Originals. I am indebted to the two anonymous peer reviewers who gave
me both positive encouragement and valuable feedback. I also would
like to thank the kind and supportive professional staff at Penn State
University Press, particularly Ellie Goodman, for guiding me through

the publication process and for turning my manuscript into a book that hopefully will be useful to scholars and students for many years to come.

Latin American Originals (LAO) is a series of primary source texts on colonial Latin America. LAO volumes are accessible editions of texts translated into English—most of them for the very first time. Of the nineteen volumes now in print, about half illuminate aspects of the Spanish invasions in the Americas during the long sixteenth century of 1494 to 1614. The others take the series in varied and exciting directions, from the forging of new Christianities to medical science. The present volume reflects both trajectories by examining the role of other European actors, specifically Germans, in the invasions of what is now Venezuela.

Taken in the chronological order of their primary texts, *Of Cannibals and Kings* (LAO 7) comes first. It presents the earliest written attempts to describe Indigenous American cultures, offering striking insight into how Europeans struggled from the very start to conceive a New World. *The Native Conquistador* (LAO 10) tells the story of the (in)famous Spanish conquest expeditions into Mexico and Central America from 1519 to 1524—but from the startlingly different perspective of a royal Indigenous dynasty, as told by the great-great-grandson of the alternative leading protagonist.

Next, chronologically, are LAOs 2, 1, and 9. *Invading Guatemala* shows how reading multiple accounts of conquest wars (in this case, Spanish, Nahua, and Maya versions of the Guatemalan conflict of the 1520s) can explode established narratives and suggest a more complex and revealing conquest story. *Invading Colombia* challenges us to view the difficult Spanish invasion of Colombia in the 1530s as more representative of conquest campaigns than the better-known assaults on the Aztec and Inca empires. It complements *The Improbable Conquest*, which presents letters written between 1537 and 1556 by Spaniards struggling—with a persistence that is improbable indeed—to establish a colony along the hopefully named Río de la Plata.

The present volume (LAO 19) and *Contesting Conquest* (LAO 12) add intriguingly to this trio. *Violent First Contact in Venezuela* introduces us to the life and writings of Nikolaus Federmann, the military commander and Welser Company agent who led the German exploration and invasion of Venezuela. The Welser Company was the only non-Iberian company contracted by the Spanish Crown to invade any region of the Americas. Federmann's account of this unique episode in early Latin American history sheds new light on the challenges and complex financial dealings behind this attempt to colonize Venezuela in the 1530s. Likewise, *Contesting Conquest* (LAO 12) offers new perspectives on Nueva Galicia's understudied early history. Indigenous witnesses and informants—their voices deftly identified, selected, and presented—guide us through the grim, messy tale of repeated efforts at conquest and colonization from the late 1520s through 1545.

LAOs 11, 3, 4, and 16 all explore aspects of the aftermath and legacy of the invasion era. *The History of the New World* offers the first English translation since 1847 of part of an Italian book of 1565 that, in its day, was a best seller in five languages. The merchant-adventurer Girolamo Benzoni mixed sharp observations and sympathy for Indigenous peoples with imaginary tales and wild histories, influencing generations of early modern readers and challenging contemporary readers to sort out fact from fable. *The Conquest on Trial* features a fictional Indigenous embassy filing a complaint in a court in Spain—the Court of Death. The first theatrical examination of the conquest published in Spain, it effectively condensed contemporary debates on colonization into one dramatic package. It contrasts well with *Defending the Conquest*, which presents a spirited, ill-humored, and polemic apologia for the Spanish Conquest, written in 1613 by a veteran conquistador. *Indigenous Life After the Conquest* presents the papers of a Nahua family, showing how family members navigated the gradual changes and challenges that swept Central Mexico in the century after the dramatic upheaval of invasion and conquest. Through Indigenous eyes, we see how a new order was built, contested, shaped, and reconfigured by Nahuas themselves.

Indigenous Life After the Conquest dovetails in many ways with volumes 5, 6, 8, and 13—which explore aspects of Spanish efforts to implant Christianity in the New World. Chronologically, *To Heaven or to Hell* leads the pack, presenting the first complete English translation of a book by Bartolomé de Las Casas. Originally published in 1552, his *Confessionary for Confessors*—soon overshadowed by his famous *Very Brief Account of the Destruction of the Indies*—was initially just as controversial; conquistadors and other Spaniards were outraged by its demand that they themselves be effectively made subject to the spiritual conquest in the New World.

Gods of the Andes presents the first English edition of a 1594 manuscript describing Inca religion and the campaign to convert native Andeans. Its Jesuit author is surprisingly sympathetic to preconquest beliefs and practices, viewing them as preparing Andeans for the arrival of the new faith. *Forgotten Franciscans* casts new light on the spiritual conquest and the conflictive cultural world of the Inquisition in sixteenth-century Mexico. Both these volumes expose wildly divergent views within the Spanish American church on native religions and how to replace them with Christianity. Complementing those books by revealing the Indigenous side of the same process, *Translated Christianities* presents religious texts translated from Nahuatl and Yucatec Maya. Designed to proselytize and ensure the piety of Indigenous parishioners, these texts show how such efforts actually contributed to the development of local Christianities.

LAOs 14, 15, and 17 take the series in bold new directions. *An Irish Rebel in New Spain* casts a sharp eye on the far-reaching intrigues of colonial and Inquisitorial politics. William Lamport, aka the Irish Zorro, rose through colonial Mexican society only to lose his life in the clutches of the Holy Office. LAO 17 explores his dramatic life, theological philosophies, and provocative writings to shed light on the cruel whimsy of (mis)fortune in a time of upheaval and instability in Spanish America. *To the Shores of Chile* presents "the Journal and History" of a Dutch expedition to Chile, bringing to more than seven the number of languages from which LAO sources have been translated. Extending the series into a new region of the Americas, it opens up a different perspective on European-Indigenous interaction, colonization, and global competition in the age of empire. *Baptism Through Incision* takes the LAO series later in time and into medical history, using an eighteenth-century Guatemalan case study to explore the fascinating intersections between faith and science in the early modern world. This first English publication of an eye-opening 1786 treatise on performing cesareans on pregnant women at the moment of their death explores anew many of the themes that are threaded through this series—empire, salvation, the female body, and knowledge as a New World battleground.

The source texts in LAO volumes are colonial-era rare books or archival documents, written in European or Mesoamerican languages. LAO authors are historians, anthropologists, art historians, geographers, and scholars of literature who have developed a specialized knowledge that allows them to locate, translate, and present these texts in a way that contributes to a scholarly understanding of the period while also making them readable for students and nonspecialists. Peter Hess is one such scholar, and his skilled presentation of a difficult text is a significant and welcome contribution to this series.

—Matthew Restall

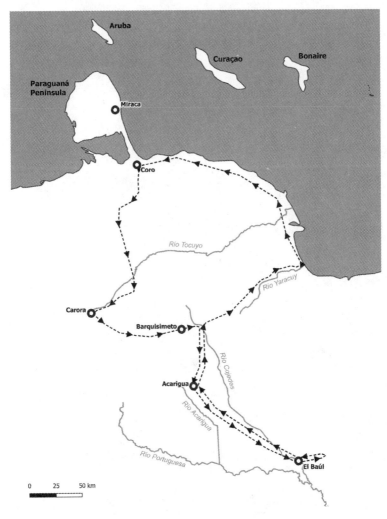

MAP Venezuela, showing the approximate itinerary of Federmann's incursion of 1530 to 1531. The text divulges little identifiable geographic information, which is why this map has to be taken as an approximation. Map courtesy of Michael Shensky, University of Texas Libraries.

The attempted colonization of Venezuela by the Welser merchant company of Augsburg, Germany, is a remarkable chapter of the colonial history of the Americas. While the participation of merchants in the Conquest was common, the Welsers, who often were referred to as Bélzares in Spanish sources, led the only foreign company that was awarded a contract by the Spanish Crown to colonize a territory in the New World. Nikolaus Federmann, aka Nicolás de Federmán (1506–1542), was a military commander appointed by the Welsers to secure their rule over Venezuela. The text presented here is a unique document that chronicles Federmann's six-month incursion into the interior of Venezuela from 1530 to 1531. It gives us insight into his strategic thinking, dissimulations, and attempts at understanding the viewpoints and motivations of the Indians. It reveals his unbridled use of force and violence but also his fears of existential threats. It documents his unshaken belief in the intrinsic preeminence of European Christians and in the righteousness of his mission.

The Welser Merchant House As Global Player

The Welser Company was one of the wealthy and influential transnational merchant-banker corporations based in southern Germany, second only to the Fugger Company, also of Augsburg. Starting in the second half of the fifteenth century, these corporations created Pan-European networks of trading, mining, manufacturing, and banking interests. The Welsers and Fuggers were among early investors in the Asian spice trade developed by the Portuguese.

The Welser Company started to engage in the Spanish trade shortly after 1500. By 1510, the Welsers had branch offices in Saragossa and Valencia,[1] and in 1525, they opened an office in Seville,[2] the Spanish port that handled all commerce with the West Indies at the time. In 1526, the Welsers established an office in Santo Domingo,[3] then the commercial and political hub of the emerging Spanish colonial empire, and started to operate plantations on Hispaniola.[4] Ambrosius Dalfinger (ca. 1500–1533), who later became the first Welser governor of Venezuela, and Georg Ehinger (1503–1537/40) were the first Welser factors in America.[5] On 12 February 1528, the Welsers received the license to bring four thousand slaves from Africa to Santo Domingo, a large number at the time. Even though the Welsers had to work through Portuguese intermediaries, as they had no ties to Africa, this transaction appears to have been lucrative for the Company.[6]

There was a scant Spanish presence in Venezuela, literally "Little Venice," before the arrival of the Welsers. Since Christopher Columbus had reported pearl banks during his third voyage, the coast of Venezuela was explored and charted in 1499 in two separate expeditions led by Alonso de Ojeda and by Vicente Yáñez Pinzón.[7] In 1521, Bartolomé de Las Casas set up a short-lived experimental reduction in Cumaná in the Tierra Firme—that is, in the Venezuelan mainland—to colonize and evangelize the region peacefully.[8] In the 1520s and perhaps earlier, the Spanish exploited pearls along the Pearl Coast, east of Cumaná, just outside of the Welser zone of conquest.[9] In his text, Federmann describes the existing Spanish practice of raiding the coast of Venezuela to capture slaves who then were forced to

1. Denzer, *Die Konquista der Augsburger Welser-Gesellschaft*, 46.
2. Denzer, "Die Welser in Venezuela," 290.
3. Häberlein, *Fuggers of Augsburg*, 80.
4. Denzer, *Die Konquista der Augsburger Welser-Gesellschaft*, 50.
5. Simmer, *Gold und Sklaven*, 35–36.
6. Tyce, "Hispano-German Caribbean," 242–44; Montenegro, "Textual and Visual Representations," 105; Denzer, *Die Konquista der Augsburger Welser-Gesellschaft*, 54.
7. Pastor Bodmer, *Armature of Conquest*, 58.
8. Orique, *To Heaven or to Hell*, 12–14.
9. Perri, "'Ruined and Lost,'" 129–61, and Warsh, *American Baroque*, 31–38.

work in mines and on plantations on the island of Hispaniola[10] [B4r; P2v]. Juan Martínez de Ampiés (d. 1533) served as the first governor of Venezuela from 1527 to 1529. He founded the city of Santa Ana de Coro on 26 July 1527, which remained the seat of colonial administration until 1578, when it was moved to Caracas.

The Welsers in Venezuela

The Welser colonial project in Venezuela was based on a contract with Emperor Charles V of Habsburg (1500–1558), who was simultaneously King Charles I of Spain.[11] The contract followed a pattern of such partnerships with nonstate actors who financed explorations and conquests without adding debt for the crown. The Burgos merchant-banker García de Lerma (ca. 1470–1532), then the governor of the neighboring Santa Marta province, persuaded the Welsers to enter the agreement.[12] The Welsers saw an opportunity to set up lucrative mining operations and perhaps to enhance their global trade network by finding a passage to the Pacific Ocean.[13] It is unlikely that the Welsers received these rights as a compensation for earlier loans to the House of Habsburg, as some claim.[14] The Welsers did not receive preferential treatment and were required to finance the expedition themselves.[15]

Technically, the *asiento* (contract) of 27 March 1528 was signed by two Welser representatives in Seville, Hieronymus Sailer (1495–1559) and Heinrich Ehinger (1484–1537), a brother of Georg Ehinger, the Welser factor in Santo Domingo, and of Ulrich Ehinger (1485–1537), a Welser agent in Spain with connections to Charles V. The Welser Company became the official contract partner only in 1531. The contract defined as the Welser zone of conquest the coastline

---

10. On the trade of Indigenous slaves in the Caribbean, see Stone, "War and Rescate."

11. Großhaupt, "Der Venezuela-Vertrag der Welser," 3.

12. Denzer, *Die Konquista der Augsburger Welser-Gesellschaft*, 51, and Großhaupt, "Der Venezuela-Vertrag der Welser," 4–6. García de Lerma is mentioned in the *asiento*.

13. Großhaupt, "Der Venezuela-Vertrag der Welser," 1.

14. Thomas, *Golden Empire*, 148–49.

15. See the German translation of the *asiento* in Simmer, *Gold und Sklaven*, 757–70.

between the Cabo de la Vela in the west, the border to the Santa Marta province, and the Cabo de Maracapana near Cumaná in the east, as well as the land to the south of the coastline.[16]

The activities of the Welser operatives in Venezuela mostly consisted of six major *entradas* (incursions) into the interior of Venezuela. The first incursion from August 1529 to May 1530 was commanded by Governor Dalfinger and explored Lake Maracaibo. Shortly after that, Federmann led an incursion to the Orinoco Basin in a southerly direction, lasting from 12 September 1530 to 17 March 1531. The English translation of Federmann's account of this incursion is featured in this book. Dalfinger's second incursion, from 9 June 1531 to 2 November 1533, advanced westward to the Magdalena River in Colombia. Dalfinger was killed on the way back to Coro on 31 May 1533, poisoned by an enemy arrow.[17] The *entrada* directed by Georg Hohermuth von Speyer, aka Jorge de Espira (1500–1540), from 13 May 1535 to 27 May 1538 followed the Eastern Cordillera of Colombia all the way to Ecuador. Federmann's second *entrada* reaching Bogotá from 1536 to 1539 will be discussed later. The final Welser *entrada*, led by Philipp von Hutten (1505–1546) and beginning on 1 August 1541, penetrated the western reaches of the Amazon Basin in southeastern Colombia and ended with the murder of Hutten and Bartholomäus VI Welser (1512–1546), the eldest son of the company executive, on 17 May 1546 on orders of the governor Juan de Carvajal (1509–1546), who in turn was executed for his involvement in the murders.

While a German company was in charge of the colony, the majority of settlers were of Spanish origin, and Spanish officials present in Coro collected taxes and ensured that the colony was administered according to Spanish law.[18] The Welsers never developed mines or plantations in Venezuela, and the venture was never profitable for the Welsers. They ceased their Venezuela activities in 1546 and closed down their operations on the island of Hispaniola in 1547, with their share of the emerging transatlantic trade never having reached significant proportions. The *asiento* formally expired in 1556.[19]

---

16. Ibid., 757.
17. Ibid., 167.
18. Tyce, "Hispano-German Caribbean," 246–48.
19. Johnson, *German Discovery*, 166–95, in particular 187–91.

It is difficult to assess the effect of Welser colonization on Venezuela. Spanish sources accused Federmann of treating his soldiers poorly and of committing unnecessary violent acts against the Indigenous nations.[20] Furthermore, new diseases were a lasting part of colonial legacy. Federmann describes the massive population loss on the island of Hispaniola [B2v], and he reports how the Ayamanes had been devastated by smallpox years before his arrival [D4v]. While the Welsers permanently changed many coastal communities where they ruled, they did not manage to establish footholds in the Orinoco Basin. There is no evidence of a full collapse of Indigenous sociopolitical structures in areas removed from the coast,[21] but we do not know how Federmann's *entrada* and brief contact affected the culture and self-understanding of the nations he encountered. The Spaniards did not return to the region until the Jesuits started to establish missions in the Middle Orinoco region around 1680.

Nikolaus Federmann and His Incursion

Nikolaus Federmann was born in the southern German city of Ulm in 1506. Little is known about his life and education before he joined the Welser Company. Like most other key Welser overseas operatives, Federmann had neither familial nor financial ties to the Welser Company.[22] In Augsburg, Federmann was given access to handwritten translations of conquistadors' reports[23] [K1r]. Much of what we know about Federmann's first journey to Venezuela is based on his own account, although some Spanish sources complement the picture. Federmann must have learned Spanish quickly, as there were no acknowledged communication problems with Spaniards.

Federmann's narration begins with his embarkment in Sanlúcar de Barrameda, Seville's port. He likely was briefed in Seville before, both at the Welser offices and at the Casa de Contratación, where the cartographer Diogo Ribeiro (d. 1533) was the keeper of the *Padrón Real*, the master map of the world that was updated with each new

---

20. Simmer, *Gold und Sklaven*, 141–44.
21. Arvelo, "Change and Persistence," 683.
22. Denzer, *Die Konquista der Augsburger Welser-Gesellschaft*, 60.
23. Johnson, *German Discovery*, 218 n. 122.

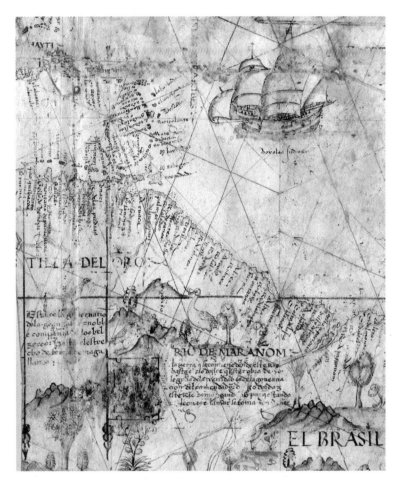

FIG. 1 Map of "Castilla de Oro." From Diogo Ribeiro, *Welser Map* (fragment), Seville, 1530. Studienbibliothek Dillingen, Mapp. 1. The five known world maps by Ribeiro all label the area of today's Venezuela "Castilla del Oro." Two of them, this one and a 1529 map held by the Anna Amalia Bibliothek Weimar, both indicate that the Welsers were governing the territory, which is why it is likely that both maps were produced for the Welsers. It is conceivable that Federmann had access to at least one of them.

report. Ribeiro created copies for maritime pilots, at least one for the Welsers. Five of these maps survive, and two of them note the Welser rule in Venezuela.

On 2 October 1529, Federmann left Sanlúcar with 123 Spanish soldiers and 24 German miners on a ship furnished by the Welser agent Ulrich Ehinger.[24] He spent at least two weeks in Santo Domingo in December 1529. As the seat of the Real Audiencia (Spanish court), founded in 1511, Santo Domingo was the base for all conquest activities at the time, where conquistadors like Federmann studied strategies that accelerated domination in other spaces in the West Indies.[25] Here, he would have also learned more about Christopher Columbus, Hernán Cortés, and Pedro Arias Dávila, all of whom Federmann mentions in his text [K1r], as well as about the recent disastrous expeditions by Lucas Vázquez de Ayllón (ca. 1480–1526) and Pánfilo de Narváez (1478–1528), which, like his own, involved backcountry explorations into inhospitable terrain.

Federmann and his crew, plus ten horses that were loaded in Santo Domingo, arrived in the recently established coastal town of Coro, the first administrative seat in Venezuela, on 8 March 1530. Governor Dalfinger appointed Federmann as his deputy, and when he went back to Santo Domingo in July, Federmann became responsible for the emerging colony. Without specific authorization, Federmann undertook an *entrada* to the interior of the territory from 12 September 1530 to 17 March 1531. According to his own calculations [P4r], he and his men traveled about 270 Spanish miles or about 1,145 kilometers. The trip was the first European exploration of the interior of Venezuela, as Federmann proudly proclaims [P4r]. The journey took him through the lands of nine different Indigenous nations he identified by name, each discussed in separate chapters.

He started out "with 110 Spaniards on foot and sixteen on horseback" as well as with 100 native carriers of supplies [C4r]. The number of carriers fluctuated greatly as many managed to escape, and new ones were forced into service along the way. Federmann refers to his fighting force as "Christians," a term that is ubiquitous in conquest narratives and reflects the multinational character of

---

24. All dates come from Federmann's own account, which are not disputed in scholarship.

25. Rojas, Samson, and Hoogland, "Indo-Hispanic Dynamics," 20.

these crews.[26] Furthermore, the term delineated the contrast with the non-Christian Other. He stopped his incursion just outside Coro for two days to organize his cohort, which indicates that the assemblage was not an organized military unit but a group of mercenaries and colonists he had recruited in Coro.

His journey led him through mountainous terrain to Barquisimeto and Acarigua. From there he ventured into the swamps of the Orinoco River Basin in a southerly direction, primarily in search of a passage to the Pacific Ocean. At that point, he encountered difficulties because of mass illness, a swampy terrain not suited for horses, and increasingly strong and hostile Indigenous nations. He was forced to return to Barquisimeto. From there, he had to choose the longer but safer route along the Yaracuy River to the Caribbean Sea and then westward along the Caribbean coast back to Coro. We do not learn the fate of the many Indians Federmann brought with him; they were likely sold as slaves.

When Federmann arrived in Coro on 13 March 1531, Governor Dalfinger had returned. Dalfinger banned Federmann from Venezuela for four years for insubordination even though there is no evidence that Federmann had been instructed not to undertake such an *entrada*.[27] Furthermore, Federmann had a conflictual relationship with the Spanish authorities, particularly with the notary Antonio de Naveros (ca. 1500–1552), whom Federmann had put in chains during the last two months of the *entrada*.[28] It is therefore possible that Dalfinger banned Federmann to appease the Spaniards. While Dalfinger left for his second *entrada* on 9 June 1531, Federmann did not leave Coro until 9 December 1531, as his fever had returned, perhaps from malaria [P4v]; he reached Santo Domingo on 18 December. He embarked on his journey to Seville on 4 April 1532, arriving on 16 June. Federmann was back in Augsburg on 31 August 1532.

Federmann likely drafted his report in 1532 or 1533 for the Welsers. They issued a new seven-year contract to Federmann on 2 October 1533.[29] On 19 July 1534, we find Federmann in Valladolid, where he was appointed governor and captain general of the Venezuela

26. Wojciehowski, *Group Identity*, 92.
27. Simmer, *Gold und Sklaven*, 140.
28. Ibid., 141–43. Federmann does not mention this occurrence in his text.
29. Ibid., 371; Großhaupt, "Der Venezuela-Vertrag der Welser," 32.

province at the request of the Welsers.[30] However, his papers were soon revoked, and Georg Hohermuth was appointed in his stead. Federmann returned to Santo Domingo on 5 December 1534 and presented his petition to become governor to the Real Audiencia the following January.[31] By 11 May 1535, Federmann was back in Coro, where Governor Hohermuth named him his deputy; he left on his *entrada* two days later.

In October of the same year, Federmann was appointed governor again, but the papers did not arrive in Coro until 24 November 1537, after being held up in Santo Domingo for more than a year. Federmann departed for his second *entrada* in early 1536. He and his men moved slowly and waited for over a year, as Federmann was still hoping that the paperwork confirming his appointment would arrive in time. In October 1537, Federmann started to move into the Cordillera Oriental of the Andes, in search of the legendary El Dorado. He entered Cundinamarca, the highlands around Bogotá, by March 1539; he is considered a cofounder of Santa Fe de Bogotá, chartered on 27 April 1539. Gonzalo Jiménez de Quesada (ca. 1496–1579) had arrived first from Santa Marta and was already established when his two competitors, Federmann and Sebastián de Belalcázar (1479/80–1551), arrived. In July 1539, the three men, Jiménez, Belalcázar, and Federmann, traveled back to Spain together, via the Magdalena Valley and Cartagena, to settle their competing claims to Cundinamarca before the emperor.[32]

Federmann arrived in Spain in early January 1540. He traveled to Ghent, where the imperial court was located at the time. There he met with Bartholomäus V Welser in June 1540 to discuss the Welser claim to Cundinamarca. However, the Council of the Indies ruled in September that Cundinamarca should belong to the Santa Marta province, thus honoring Jiménez's claim. Furthermore, Welser accused Federmann of insubordination and embezzlement and had him arrested. Emperor Charles V ordered Federmann extradited to Spain, where he was to testify against the Welsers before the Council of the Indies.[33] Federmann arrived in Madrid in February 1541. His

---

30. Simmer, *Gold und Sklaven*, 258–60.
31. Montenegro, "Textual and Visual Representations," 95.
32. Francis, *Invading Colombia*, 101–2, 110 n. 36.
33. Simmer, *Gold und Sklaven*, 377.

conflict with the Welsers remained unresolved, and furthermore, the Spanish Inquisition suspected him of being a Lutheran. Federmann died on the twenty-first or twenty-second of February 1542, in jail in Valladolid, under unknown circumstances.

The Text: Who Wrote It and for Whom?

The only known source for Federmann's text, which was used for this translation, is a posthumously printed version from 1557, issued by Sigmund Bund, a minor printer in the Alsatian town of Haguenau. Unlike comparable texts, Federmann's report was never reprinted in the popular compilations that appeared around 1600, like those by Theodor de Bry, Levinus Hulsius, and Johann Ludwig Gottfried. Federmann's book was not published again in any version until the nineteenth century. The dedication of the book was signed by Hans Kiffhaber (or Kiefhaber) of Ulm, who identified himself as Federmann's brother-in-law. We do not know how Kiffhaber gained access to the text nor how he was related to the printer Bund.

German scholarship classifies the text as a travelogue, presumably because it is framed as a travel narrative, as a diary,[34] or as an "adventurous travel narrative."[35] No doubt with an eye to the German book market, the subtitle of the printed book promised "a beautiful and entertaining story," and Kiffhaber in his dedication pitched the text as a travel and adventure narrative that "is very amusing and entertaining to read" [A2v]. Some features of the text favor this view, such as the chapter headings and summaries that emphasize the adventurous plot elements. These features that promote the text as a travel narrative were not present in Federmann's original report.

Some suggest that Kiffhaber was the German translator of the text,[36] without explaining how he had access to a hypothetical Spanish-language text and leaving aside the fact that there is no reason to believe that he could read Spanish. It is unlikely that Kiffhaber made significant changes,[37] as he had neither the language skills nor

---

34. Arvelo, "Change and Persistence," 681.
35. Montenegro, "Conquistadors and Indians," 273.
36. Harbsmeier, *Wilde Völkerkunde*, 89.
37. Wagner, "Nikolaus Federmanns Jndianische Historia," 165.

the necessary cultural and political information about the Indian or Spanish colonial contexts needed to draft or edit this text.

A closer examination reveals that the text at its core was modeled after the *probanza de mérito*, literally "proof of merit"—that is, a report that described and justified actions taken by conquistadors in colonial settings. The Spaniards pursued an explicit policy that ordered conquistadors to provide an account of their explorations, conquests, and settlements but that also allowed authors to promote their own accomplishments. Early conquistadors typically chronicled their exploits in letters to the Spanish Crown, starting with the famous letter Columbus wrote in 1493 on his journey back from the West Indies. Equally renowned are the letters by Cortés to Charles V, known as the *Cartas de Relación*. With the founding of the Council of the Indies in 1524, the reporting of conquest activities was formalized administratively.

Federmann certainly was informed of these obligations and knew that each commander was required to submit an account of his actions in Indian lands [K1r; P3r]. He was familiar with the generic expectations of the *probanza de mérito* and used this model for his own account. The text shows that Federmann was eager to prove that he performed within the Spanish rules of engagement. Federmann himself states that a Spanish notary, presumably Naveros, traveled along on the journey and took notes [P3r]. Kiffhaber repeats this assertion in his dedication [A2v]. It has been suggested that Naveros completed a full draft of a report, which is not extant, on which Federmann's text is based.[38] It is more likely, however, that a full report never existed and that Naveros merely drafted more or less extensive notes. Others claim that the report was part of a letter Naveros and Alsono Vázquez de Acuña wrote to the Spanish Crown on 8 October 1533.[39] Only a part of that letter is concerned with Federmann's *entrada*; moreover, the text is considerably shorter, and it has a different structure and focus than Federmann's German-language text.[40] When this letter was drafted, Federmann was already back in Germany and thus had

---

38. Ribas, *Testimonios de la conciencia lingüistica*, 79, and Wagner, "Nikolaus Federmanns Jndianische Historia," 166.

39. Simmer, *Gold und Sklaven*, 125–26.

40. Márquez, *Descubrimiento y conquista de Venezuela*, 2, 274–313.

no knowledge of it. Therefore, it stands to reason that Federmann, at most, had access to notes drafted by Naveros.

Federmann himself claims that he translated his text into German [P3r–v], and Kiffhaber confirms this [A2v]. Federmann asserts that he added many descriptions and "many aspects of the manners and customs of the Indian lands" that otherwise "would be entirely incomprehensible and would have been much too obscure for those to whom such things are entirely alien" [P3v]. Furthermore, he uses a large number of Spanish terms, like *cacique, naturales, pueblo,* or *bohío,* which he then explains for his German readers. We also have to consider that Federmann had Naveros's preliminary account (which he called "Relation," from the Spanish *relación*) sent back to Coro with a messenger once he had reached the coast [P3r], and he probably did not have access to it after that. Additionally, at that point, Naveros was in chains, so he was no longer taking notes. The translation hypothesis is thus not tenable, and we have to conclude that Federmann is the author rather than just translator of this text. Federmann's own claim to merely have translated the text likely was a part of an authentication strategy. Asserting that a Spanish notary drafted the report created an aura of detached neutrality and objectivity, thus validating the account and giving the appearance of Federmann's friendly cooperation with Spanish authorities.

This leaves the question of the intended audience. Circumstances indicate that Federmann wrote the German-language text as a report for the Welsers to justify his actions,[41] given that he was banned from the Venezuela colony by the Welser governor Dalfinger. Throughout the text, Federmann highlights his own actions while discounting a Spanish role in his *entrada.* His use of pronouns, which is preserved in this translation, supports this claim. The text was written in the first person, often reverting to the singular form even when including his men. He used the second-person form to emphatically justify his handling of difficult situations. This wording allows for the conclusion that he was addressing his superiors at the Welser Company. At the same time, he barely mentions the Spanish officials and clergy—and never by name—thus marginalizing their role in his *entrada.* It is evident that authors like Federmann used such

---

41. Denzer, *Die Konquista der Augsburger Welser-Gesellschaft,* 77, and Wagner, "Nikolaus Federmanns Jndianische Historia," 166, 168.

reports as vehicles for their own social and political advancement.[42] By claiming that his text was a mere translation, he glosses over the fundamental disagreements and deep-seated conflicts he had with the Spanish officials regarding his *entrada*.

As mentioned before, Federmann returned to Augsburg on 31 August 1532 and signed a seven-year contract renewing his employment with the Welser Company on 2 October 1533. Federmann likely used this report to secure the new contract and therefore drafted and presented it to the Welser Company prior to October 1533. While mostly boosting his own accomplishments in the text, he identifies the Welsers as his masters five times, although only in passing [A3v; B3r; C2r; C2v; P4v]. He also does not explain how his actions benefitted the Welser Company and why he made no effort to set up the mining operations desired by the Welsers. Once back in Venezuela, Federmann no longer had an incentive to finish a report in German. When he returned to Europe after his second incursion of 1536 to 1539, his focus was entirely on having his claim to Cundinamarca confirmed by the Spanish Crown and on defending himself against allegations of misconduct levied both by the Welsers and by Spanish officials. We have no record of Federmann returning to Augsburg after his second *entrada*.

It is unknown why the text was printed only in 1557, fifteen years after Federmann's death. It is conceivable that Federmann had plans to publish it himself but did not have the opportunity to do so, which is why he left a copy of the manuscript with Kiffhaber, his brother-in-law. Kiffhaber may have been motivated to publish Federmann's manuscript by the commercial success of other narratives describing travel to the West Indies.[43] The title of the published book and the dedication were designed to appeal to a noble or urban German reader seeking a pleasurable adventure text. However, the book, which was produced without illustrations, did not meet these expectations and never became a commercial success.

---

42. Brendecke, "Der 'oberste Kosmograph und Chronist Amerikas,'" 360.
43. Ribas, *Testimonios de la conciencia lingüistica*, 76.

The Translation

The goal of this project is to present in its entirety a reliable as well as readable translation that accurately represents Federmann's original text written in Early New High German. I used the original 1557 imprint at the Herzog August Bibliothek Wolfenbüttel for my translation. As this text is not primarily a literary work, this translation prioritizes an accurate rendition of the events and circumstances to make it usable for historians, anthropologists, and scholars of different fields, as well as for students. To achieve this objective, a number of compromises had to be made.

Federmann's text is of an extraordinary syntactic complexity. His sentences typically consist of numerous clauses that are boxed into each other. Erratic punctuation makes it difficult to recognize syntactic structures. As it was neither desirable nor possible to render this complexity in a modern English translation, I broke up Federmann's long sentences, which sometimes required a slight reorganization of the information presented in the original. I preserved the division into chapters from the 1557 imprint, including titles and summaries, and added chapter numbers. As the 1557 imprint used paragraph breaks quite sparingly, I added numerous breaks throughout the text to enhance its readability.

Federmann's choices of vocabulary present numerous problems. He uses technical Spanish language specific to the conquest and colonization of Latin America. The text also bears traits of German chancery texts and of German legal language of the time. One such term is "peinlich fragen" [M3r; M4r; O4r], literally "asking painfully," indicating interrogation under torture.[44] Federmann describes the houses of the Caquetíos near Barquisimeto in a brief ethnographic excursus in which he used the term "haußvolck" to describe the number of inhabitants of a house [N4v], a legal term designating all members of a household, including servants. When Federmann and his men arrived in the first village of the Jirajaras, he found its inhabitants "in rüwiger possession" [C4v], which has been previously translated as "in repentant procession."[45] Rather, the term is rooted in legal language, referring to a right of possession based on habitual

---

44. Wagner, "Nikolaus Federmanns Jndianische Historia," 166.
45. Harbsmeier, "Gifts and Discoveries," 401.

law, and the adjective "ruhig," literally "quiet," indicated that this right was undisputed or undisturbed. This term does not imply a contrite or apologetic attitude by the cacique; rather it describes an assured posture, hence my translation, "in a confident pose."

Federmann includes a significant number of words of Spanish origin, like *edificias* [B2v] for "buildings," *multitud* [B3r] for "large number," *costa* [B3v] for "coast," and *descubridor* [K1r] for "explorer." I preserved those words that can be used in English, like *pueblo*, *cacique*, or *Indios*, while I used English equivalents for others. Since Federmann uses the word *Indio* when referring to the natives, I used it in the translation as well. The usage of some words is less obvious, like his description of a storm as "fortuna oder wetter" [P4v], referring to bad weather or a storm. The phrase is based on the Spanish nautical expression *correr fortuna*, riding out a storm on a ship. The truncated form "fortuna" is not very meaningful in a German-language text, as it easily could be misread as "fortune" or "fate."

A unique stylistic feature of Federmann's text is the pairing of two mostly synonymous terms, generally one in German and the second one frequently derived from Spanish. I decided to preserve this idiosyncratic feature to render some of the flavor of Federmann's text. Examples are "Schiffer oder Marineros" [A4v; Q1v] for "sailors or mariners, "Naturales oder einwoner" [B2v] for "natives or inhabitants," "Confederation oder verbündtnüs" [E2r] for "confederation or alliance," and "Presentes vnd schanckungen" [E3r] for "presents and gifts." The most common pairings by far are "Pueblos oder flecken" for "pueblos or villages" and "Cacique oder Herr" for "cacique or leader." Federmann repeatedly refers to the redundancies built into his text, which is why I preserved them in my translation.

Only a handful of geographic names in Venezuela can be identified, like the modern cities of Coro, Miraca, Barquisimeto, and Acarigua, as well as some rivers. Geographic names that can be attributed, including those in Spain, off the coast of Africa, and in the Caribbean, appear in their modern spelling in the translation; those that cannot be identified follow Federmann's spelling. None of the locations in the Orinoco Basin past Barquisimeto and Acarigua can be established because Spaniards did not enter this area again until the late seventeenth century, which is why reconstructing Federmann's itinerary in the Orinoco Basin past Acarigua is elusive.

Likewise, only some of the nine native nations Federmann discusses in detail and others he mentioned in passing can be identified today, such as the Caquetíos, who play a dominant role in Federmann's narrative. The Jirajaras were part of a known Jirajaran family of languages that became extinct as early as the seventeenth century. There is a degree of uncertainty about the various nations Federmann describes, as most Indigenous nations could not maintain their cultural and linguistic identities after colonization. For some of the nations, Federmann is the only person ever to write about them, and many histories of early Venezuela rely on Federmann's account.[46] The translation uses the modern names of the nations that are commonly used today. Unfortunately, Federmann did not add ethnographic descriptions in spite of his repeated promises in his text.

Federmann's use of measurements is explained in footnotes, with the exception of the mile. The German mile is around 7.5 kilometers, with significant regional variations, while the Spanish mile, or *legua*, usually measures only 4.24 kilometers. The distances that can be verified today generally indicate that Federmann used the Spanish mile as a unit, as the two following examples show. He gives the distance between Sanlúcar de Barrameda and Lanzarote as 300 miles or 1,272 kilometers, the actual distance being 1,093 kilometers as the crow flies. The distance he indicates between the island of La Gomera and Santo Domingo is 1,300 miles or 5,512 kilometers, the actual distance being 5,444 kilometers. Federmann thus gave distances in Spanish miles, although his numbers have to be taken with a grain of salt.

What Federmann's Text Tells Us About the Conquest

A look at the themes in Federmann's text offers compelling evidence that he set up his narrative as a *probanza de mérito*, largely evidenced by his implied references to the *requerimiento* [D1r; D3v–D4r; E3r]. The *requerimiento* was a legal text that had to be read to the Indigenous people at the time of first contact to establish Spanish sovereignty; it served as a standard tool of subjugation. The 1528 contract between the Welsers and Emperor Charles V required its use in Venezuela upon first contact. It was originally drafted in

46. Most recently, Rosas González, "Población indígena."

1512 by the Spanish jurist Juan López de Palacios Rubios. Federmann presented himself as the emperor's rightful deputy [D1r] who could command the same kind of respect. He internalized the perspective of the *requerimiento* in that he believed that the natives owed him obedience and that he, through the document, possessed the right to give commands and orders to the natives. The conversion of the Indians to Catholicism and the mandatory instruction in the Christian faith, also part of the *requerimiento*, is discussed only once [D4r]. Federmann voices a subtle criticism of the efficacy of forced conversion, as opposed to instilling faith over time, which probably would not have played well in a Spanish context.

The dynamic of coercion and seduction, which is evident in Federmann's account, was inscribed into the *requerimiento*: "The primary means of coercion are military threats; those of seduction are gifts, trade opportunities, and pledges of political support."[47] This approach of simultaneously offering "friendship" and threatening the use of force was operative throughout his *entrada*. The concept of friends and friendship in a legal sense designated peaceful, contractual relations, which were asymmetrical in this context. "Friendship," therefore, described a nonreciprocal relationship demanding nonviolent submission to Spanish rule and servitude to Federmann and his men.

As his mission became increasingly difficult, Federmann resorted to acts of extreme violence and terror to maintain the upper hand, like torturing and executing hostages, massacring villagers, and burning down villages that were fully inhabited. Federmann's violence was staged theatrically, as he drew his power from the fear he instilled in the native population. While not completely concealing his violence in his text, Federmann tones down the descriptions of his actions and always justifies them as strategic necessities.

Federmann grasped that the Indigenous communities he encountered were highly localized with distinct languages and cultures and that they did not see themselves as part of larger entities, as was the norm in most conquest situations.[48] The nations he encountered lived in villages and were organized locally but did not have higher political authorities. The Orinoco Basin thus posed a particular

---

47. Ferguson and Whitehead, "Violent Edge of Empire," 7.
48. Restall, *Seven Myths*, 141, and Scaramelli and Scaramelli, "Roles of Material Culture," 139.

challenge to conquerors because the Indigenous nations were largely unconnected and isolated and rarely had centralized forms of social organization.[49]

Federmann frequently comments on the resulting communication problems and the need for interpreters he could trust [G1v]. Because of the established relationship with the Caquetíos around Coro, communicating in their language was not an issue. He tried to acquire an interpreter for each new nation he encountered. In more remote areas in the Orinoco Basin, the absence of trusted interpreters could result in dicey situations [F4r]. At one point, Federmann had to rely on a chain of five interpreters, and he himself notes that at each step something would be added or subtracted so that the outcome would be very different from what he had said originally [G1v].

Gifting was an integral part of the system of communication, and conquistadors starting with Columbus were very conscious of the significance of gifts as part of their conquest strategy.[50] Federmann was a "veritable expert in negotiating gifts as a means of exercising violent colonial power."[51] He carefully chose gifts to influence the actions of his adversaries. His gifts were of little value to him but novel and desirable to the natives [D1v; G3v; J3r; L2r]. He also gave and received human beings as presents [E4r; K3r; L3r]. Federmann tried to conceal his desire for gold so the Indians would give it more freely without expecting much in return [J2r]. He acknowledged that not every gift he received was part of a submission ritual but may have been given by natives "out of good will, solely to demonstrate their own magnificence" [G4r].

Unfortunately, Federmann gives us little ethnographic information. He mostly discusses native settlements, battle habits, and foods, which is information relevant to his *entrada*. Natives are not described as wild and uncivilized, just as adversaries who had to be subjugated or overcome. On four occasions he casually mentions that some natives engaged in anthropophagy but never used this practice as evidence for their inhumanity nor as justification for their enslavement [C4v; F3r–v; G1v; G4r]. He is greatly concerned with how and what the natives thought, and he likes to speculate how

49. Scaramelli and Scaramelli, "Roles of Material Culture," 139.
50. Vilches, "Columbus's Gift," 201–25.
51. Harbsmeier, "Gifts and Discoveries," 400.

they might have perceived him. Oddly, Federmann does not spend a lot of time discussing the Indigenous communities' weapons. They definitely used bows and arrows and perhaps blowguns. He also mentions that they threw rocks and used a clublike weapon.

Similarly, Federmann in his landscape descriptions does not portray a land of plenty that was ready to be colonized and settled, as Columbus had done. Instead, landscapes are depicted to justify his actions and illustrate the conditions of his advancement and survival. His only projections are driven by his obsessive desire to find access to the Pacific and to chase suspected fabulous wealth in the mysterious hinterland.

Much has been written about the question of why small cohorts of European mercenaries could prevail over much larger groups of native warriors.[52] Federmann reflects on this issue, confidently adding himself to a list of illustrious conquistadors who had undergone similar experiences [J4v–K1v]. Weapons played an important role. Federmann repeatedly stresses how advantageous horses were to him in battle, particularly in open fields [H4r; M3v]. He claims that the natives had an innate fear of horses, as they had never encountered the animals before [D1v; G2v]. The crossbow was a more powerful and accurate weapon than the bow and arrow of the Indians [M1v]. His most important weapon, however, remained the sword, which was very effective in close combat, both on horseback and on foot [H4r; M1v; M3v]. The arquebus played a subordinate role, as it was mentioned only once in passing [D3r]. Likewise, dogs were mentioned only once and not in a fighting capacity [O4v]; if they had a fighting role, Federmann does not reveal it. Finally, Federmann also acknowledges the role of disease. He reports that the Ayamanes could not put up resistance because they had been hit by an epidemic some years back, possibly smallpox that had been brought to the Americas by the Spaniards [D4v].

While we can only infer what acceptable norms of warfare were in the local context, Federmann and his men must have violated them to his advantage. For instance, Federmann burned houses and villages with villagers still hiding in them [J2r; K2v–K3r; M2r; O1v; O2v]. The fact that natives were hiding in their houses may indicate that they considered their houses safe zones in times of war. Furthermore,

---

52. For more on this issue, see Restall, *Seven Myths*, particularly 44–63.

Federmann targeted Indigenous leaders, as he believed natives would stop fighting once their leader was injured or killed [K1v; M1v; O2r]. Federmann reflected on norms of war on one occasion. "This is why [the natives] often said to us that we do not know how to wage war because we run close to the men right away and confuse them" [K1v]. The natives engaged in battle from a distance, while Federmann's men drove right into the crowds with their horses, killing their adversaries with swords in close combat, thus gaining an unfair advantage from the native point of view. Furthermore, Spanish records and later chronicles, particularly the account by Bartolomé de las Casas, allege that the methods of subjugation by Federmann and the Welser Company were exceptionally brutal and excessive.[53] Federmann suspended European military conventions as well in favor of "asymmetrical combat tactics" in order to compensate for the imbalance in the number of fighters.[54]

Other strategic advantages were only implied in Federmann's narrative, like being prepared for an encounter with natives who never had seen Europeans, while natives were caught off guard by the appearance of European aliens. Federmann understood that this advantage was diminished once natives were warned of his arrival ahead of time [D2r; D2v; H3r], although an early notification also could be helpful if the nation was not hostile. He and his men were able to fight without regard for seasonality and agricultural demands for manpower.[55] Federmann could rely on a mobile strike force without attachments and therefore did not have to allocate resources for the control of land or people; in contrast, the Indians struggled to protect their women, children, villages, and harvests. This need dictated the local strategic planning, which is confirmed by Federmann's frequent descriptions of natives secretly leaving their villages or evacuating women and children to safety before waging war.

Federmann also took advantage of disunity among native nations. He actively courted several nations by promising support and forging

53. Denzer, *Die Konquista der Augsburger Welser-Gesellschaft*, 26–27, 195–204; Montenegro, "Textual and Visual Representations," 175–221; Las Casas, *Account*, 64–68. For the list of Spanish sources, see Denzer, *Gold und Sklaven*, 791–821. Some of the Spanish critique refers to his second stay in Venezuela from 1536 to 1539 as well as to other Welser leaders, like Ambrosius Dalfinger.

54. Mendoza and Harder, "Mythologies of Conquest," 204.

55. Hassig, "Aztec and Spanish Conquest," 96.

alliances against neighboring nations [D3v; F4v; J4v]. The manipulation of information and deception served as additional strategies. In his view, the Indians thought the Europeans to be immortal, which is why he tried to conceal illness, injury, or death among his men [F2r–v; H1r]. He generally avoided displaying weaknesses and vulnerabilities. The Indians were masters at dissimulation as well, as Federmann notes [L1v; N2v].

Finally, Federmann's text also gives us insight into the agendas of the various stakeholders in the colonization of Venezuela. Federmann does not relate his conflicts with the Spanish civil servants, whose job was to limit the agency of military actors, to assert the fiscal interests of the Spanish Crown, and to build up a Spanish civil administration as "the era of the conquistador, private entrepreneurship, and the possibility of unbridled, unmonitored private gain was coming to an end."[56] Federmann found himself in the middle of this paradigm shift: while he acted as a free agent, his activities were suspiciously monitored and recorded by Spanish officials. The Catholic Church, another important stakeholder in the conquest, is also remarkably absent from Federmann's account.

The 1528 *asiento* proves that the Welsers were interested in mining, plantation agriculture, and general trade. The governors and conquistadors, who shared in the financial burdens of the colonial enterprise and had only time-limited contracts, were not incentivized to implement the Welsers' long-term plans. Instead, they were interested in recouping their losses by pillaging native villages.[57] Therefore, implementing the Welser agenda was a low priority for Federmann but also for other Welser officials like Dalfinger. Federmann, and with him all of the Welser governors, showed no interest in the long-term viability of the colony and sabotaged the Welser plans to set up mines in Venezuela.[58] Federmann's relationship with Dalfinger appears to have been tense, as they were competing both for leadership in the colony and also for the potential riches it had to offer. Neither the Welsers nor their operatives met their objectives, and the Welser colonial project failed in every regard.

---

56. Adorno and Pautz, *Alvar Núñez Cabeza de Vaca*, 3:310.
57. Denzer, *Die Konquista der Augsburger Welser-Gesellschaft*, 67.
58. Ibid., 79–81, contradicting Hinz, "Spanish-Indian Encounters," 22.

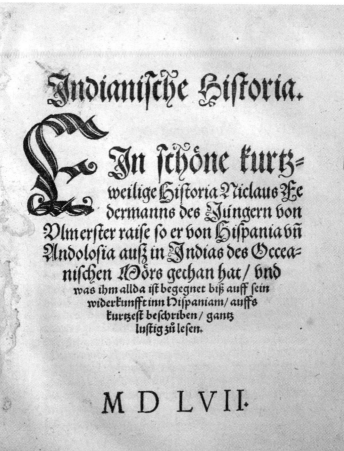

FIG. 2 Title page of Nikolaus Federmann's *Jndianische Historia: EJn schöne kurtzweilge Historia Niclaus Federmanns des Jüngern von Ulm erster raise* (Haguenau: Sigmund Bund, 1557). Herzog August Bibliothek Wolfenbüttel, 180.8 Quod. (4).

Indian History. A beautiful and entertaining story of the first journey by Nikolaus Federmann the Younger of Ulm, which he did from Spain and Andalusia to the Indies of the Atlantic Ocean, what happened to him there up to his return to Spain, described most briefly, and entertaining to read.
MDLVII.

[A2r] To the noble and mighty Johann Wilhelm von Laubenberg, from the Laubenberg castle at Wagegg, counsel to His Roman Royal Majesty and my gracious squire.[59]

Dear Gracious Squire, first off I eagerly offer my services, with hopes of all the best from God. I learned that Your Lordship are an exceptional lover and investigator of antiquities but also of those things that have emerged miraculously in our times by means of ocean navigation, through the providence of God Almighty, leading to the discovery of new islands that one calls the New World. More of these are still emerging, with many gifts of gold, gemstones, precious woods, spices, and other items. From this the clemency, goodness, and love of God for humankind can be discerned and should be taken to heart with praise and gratefulness. Without a doubt, God Almighty concealed something larger underneath, which will appear before the Day of the Lord for the benefit of all of us, as we hope. In my estimation, Your Lordship, using your highly capable intellect, thought about and observed these things long before me.

[A2v] A number of those who experienced the abovementioned New World in great danger, through difficult travels, and at considerable expense also wrote great books about it where they revealed wondrous things. Likewise, my late brother-in-law Nikolaus Federmann of Ulm wanted to explore the New World as well at different times on behalf of and with a mandate from of several masters who wanted this explored. Thus he twice traveled across the ocean to the Indies. He recorded his first journey, what happened to him and to his fellow travelers and what he saw and experienced from day to day in a notebook in the Spanish language, through a Spanish notary who

59. Johann Wilhelm von Laubenberg zu Wagegg (1511–1563) had no known connection to Federmann nor to Johann Kiffhaber.

traveled along,[60] as was required by His Imperial Majesty. Then he translated it into German and retold it. It is very amusing and entertaining to read.

As I learned that Your Lordship desired to read it as well, and inasmuch as it is useful and beneficial to humankind, I resolved to send it to you, my Dear and Gracious Squire, as you are a notable admirer and explorer of hidden things and of God's miracles, with the ardent request that Your Lordship may accept it from me favorably, as I wish to offer you more such favors. With this, I faithfully commend Your Lordship, with all of yours, to our Lord Jesus Christ. Dated in Ulm in the month of May of the year 1555.

Your very eager Hans Kiffhaber, citizen of Ulm.

[Chapter 1] About the departure of Nikolaus Federmann the Younger from Spain to the Indies, and what he encountered on this journey. Also what he saw and learned about the islands, the peoples, their manners and customs, in what physical danger he and his people were in the process, and how much they endured until their arrival in the city of Coro. [A3r]
On the second day of October of the year 1529, I, Nikolaus Federmann the Younger from Ulm, boarded a ship in Sanlúcar de Barrameda,[61] a seaport in Spain located in the province of [A3v] Andalusia. The ship was entrusted to me as captain by Mr. Ulrich Ehinger on behalf of Mr. Bartholomäus Welser and Company. I had the command over the ship, along with 123 Spanish soldiers and 24 German miners, in order to sail to the country of Venezuela, which is located on the huge Atlantic Ocean. Governance and control over it was ordered to be transferred to the said Welsers, my masters, by His Roman Imperial Majesty. I also was to assist Ambrosius Dalfinger of Ulm, who was governor and administrator of the government and authority there.

On the twenty-third day after our departure, during stormy weather and after two worrisome events, we reached an island called Lanzarote, one of the seven islands called the Canary Islands, located three hundred miles[62] from Spain. Because of headwinds, we needed

---

60. The notary was likely Antonio de Naveros. There is no record of such notations today.

61. The port of Seville.

62. Federmann uses the Spanish mile that measures 4.24 km (see introduction).

twenty-three days, as already mentioned, for a ship journey that normally takes eight to ten days at most. We lacked water so we were forced to fill up with water on this island. Although this island is subject to the Spanish kingdom, there is only one city built on it that is inhabited by Christians, located in the east and named Lanzarote like the island. As strong winds prevented us from reaching this city and port, we traveled to a port called Rubicón that is located to the north toward midnight,[63] where we would be able to find water, according to information from sailors.

I went on land with ten men, among them four Germans, [A4r] without being aware of any enemies, as nobody usually lived in the area. To our misfortune and according to God's will, there was a severe drought on this island at the time, as it had not rained in a long time. Arabs from Berbery, located seventeen miles across from the island, were granted the right to live in one location on the island and to graze and lead to pasture their cattle, goats, and camels. From there, they filled their contracts in Berbery and conducted their business activities and transactions with their cattle and dairy products, such as milk and cheese. They paid a tribute to the captain of the island to obtain the permission to do so. They brought said cattle to this port of Rubicón, where we had landed for the sake of water, which was lacking in places where the Arabs ordinarily watered their cattle. When they became aware of us, they believed that we were Frenchmen.

Just around that time, there was a war between Spain and France,[64] and many French ships, an entire armada, were present on this island and on surrounding ones. They lay in wait for ships that sailed from Spain to the Indies in order to overpower and rob them. This is why around eighty Arabs or Moriscos had assembled. As we were looking for water neither worrying about them nor anticipating their gathering, they assaulted us from an elevation about ten paces away.[65] They threw large rocks at us from there, which they handled with skill and which are their most trusted weapons. They are small people

63. Using times of day to indicate direction was common. Midnight here indicates north.

64. The war between France and the House Habsburg over the control of northern Italy, 1526–30.

65. A "Schritt" (pace), literally one normal walking step, was derived from the Roman *gradus*, measuring 2 1/2 *pedes* (feet) or about 75 cm.

but able to run fast toward and away from men, leaping like deer. As we were completely unprepared for this skirmish, they inflicted great damage on us and injured many of us [A4v] with the rocks. I was among those hurt, as I was seriously injured on my head. The Arabs overpowered us and pulled us apart. We were forced to separate, as we could no longer endure the rocks and also had no weapons with which we could have inflicted damage on them from this distance.

While they pressed us hard, and we were unable to defend ourselves, we managed to reach a hill on the opposite side. As we left the valley and climbed the hill to gain an advantage, the Arabs followed us and surrounded us on three sides. After throwing and punching for a long time, which we did on both sides, two Germans and one Spaniard among my men were stabbed to death, and the remainder of my people were seriously wounded. I was impaired by a thrown rock (as mentioned before) and also by a rapier, both wounds impacting my head. In addition I was captured by the Arabs along with two Spaniards. Two Germans and two Spaniards were able to flee to the coast, where the small boat that had taken us to shore was waiting for us. The Arabs followed those who were escaping to the shore and also threw rocks from a hill at those sitting in the small boat, wounding two sailors or mariners. My men were unable to stay at the shore and to save those four men; rather they were forced to withdraw into the ocean until the rocks thrown by the Arabs could no longer reach them. This is why the four fleeing men had to get into the ocean water and had to swim to the small boat, which they reached only with a great effort. One of them was hit by a rock while swimming. He would have drowned if those in the small boat had not saved him quickly while risking their own lives.

[B1r] The Arabs who had captured us led us to a cave where they kept us hidden because they were worried that those in the ship would find out what had happened and would attempt to wrest us away from them and free us with force. As the Arabs who had captured us had hoped to receive rescat[66] or ransom for our release, they spared us. I let them know that I wanted to communicate about this with the captain of the ship (I concealed from them that the captain was myself). They should consent to that and let me go to the ship

66. "Rescate" (rescat) is often referred to a payment for slaves.

and keep the other two captives as hostages until I returned. They did not agree to let me go free and to return to the ship. However, they allowed me to write a letter to the ship in this matter and to reveal my opinion to the captain. They wanted to send a signal to the ship that they should send someone on land to pick up a letter, with the conditions that I had to pledge not to reveal where we were being held captive and that not more than two men would come on land from the ship.

This came to pass. In response to my letter, two men came from the ship. One of them was a barber who could dress our wounds, and the other a Greek who knew the Arabic language. Thus we had full knowledge of what the Arabs were saying about us in their language among each other, without them being aware of that. I also wrote to the ship that they should leave the same night and sail to the proper city and port of Lanzarote, where the Christians lived. They should inform the governor about what had transpired so that he could quickly arrange our rescue over land. As the night set in, [B1v] I told the Arabs that the captain wanted to know from them what kind or how much ransom payment they demanded for our release. Thereon they deliberated for a long time as they believed that they could collect a large rescat or ransom for us. They envisioned two hundred ducats[67] for each of us. As we contested this expensive ransom payment, they resolved to trade all three of us together for two hundred ducats so that the governor of the island would not have an opportunity to forestall our captivity because of long delays. We had good knowledge about all their plans through the Greek mentioned above.

The Arabs got back to the shore of the ocean in the morning, where they had left the ship in the port the evening before. They intended to collect the rescat and ransom that the captain was going to send on land, as we had given them to understand, but they found that the ship had already departed. When they pointed that out to us, we feigned surprise and tried to explain the reasons for their departure after thinking about it long and hard. We said that we believed that during the past night, strong winds had come up and that the men did not feel comfortable staying in a port they did not know and

---

67. A *ducado* was a highly valued gold coin with a weight of 3.6 g (23 3/4 carat) and rated at 375 *maravedíes*.

that they rather sailed out into the open sea for their own safety to await future developments out on the ocean. In reality, we awaited help on land, each side thus waiting for what they assumed was going to happen, until the fourth day.

Finally, a number of the captain's men arrived riding camels, which they use on this island. They took us out of the Arabs' hands and accompanied us to the island's governor named Sancho de Her-rera.[68] [B2r] At his request, I told him the story of our imprisonment and the reasons for our arrival in this unusual place. After he heard from me at length, he ordered the Arabs to be pursued and brought back to him as prisoners. I did not enjoy the punishment adminis-tered to them any less than the compensation we received from him for the unlawful losses we had suffered. This governor showed me good treatment and nursed me to health. He also supplied us with provisions against payment. I stayed there until the next day to dress my wounds and those of the other injured men and also to take care of the needs of the sick ones. Then I sailed to another island called La Gomera, twelve miles away, where I arrived happily the next day. I anchored there for three days and provided the ship with wood, water, and meat according to our needs. It is almost the furthest island among the seven islands that are called the Canary Islands, and almost all ships stop there.

From there, I embarked on my journey to Santo Domingo. From the island of La Gomera, I still had 1,300 miles to travel ahead of me. Thus we reached the port of Santo Domingo still during this month of December of the year 1529. There is no need to mention the other islands we encountered and saw on the way before we reached Santo Domingo, as we did not disembark at any of them. However, I still want to mention that we sailed 900 miles from La Gomera before we saw land again. This passage is the greatest gulf of the Atlantic Ocean, and so far no larger gulf in any place of the world [B2v] has been discovered or navigated where one can travel longer without reaching land. The Portuguese seafarers who sail to India and all the way to the Moluccas travel probably further and more remotely, and with great effort and danger, but they see land after eight days at most.

68. Sancho de Herrera (1442–1534) was the governor of Lanzarote.

I arrived on this island called Hispaniola, but the city is called Santo Domingo. It is very beautifully built and has ornate streets and buildings. It also has a strong and well-fortified citadel and a very good port. On this island, which has a circumference of five hundred miles, there are many towns and cities that are inhabited by Christians, but Santo Domingo is the principal city and the best on all these islands. There is no need to write about the manner and morals of the natives or inhabitants, for it is a country that is known to have been conquered and occupied by Christians forty years ago. They are a loudly screaming people, as are those in Coro, as you will hear later, and a naked people of the same skin tone. The natives or inhabitants of this island, who owned and ruled this island before the Christians arrived there, now do not inhabit any towns of their own. Rather, they are complete subjects of the Christians and serve the Christians, as many as those who still live with them.[69]

However, there are not many of them left. As I heard, five hundred thousand Indios or inhabitants lived on the land throughout the island, in a number of nations and speaking a number of languages, when the Christians first found the island forty years ago, as mentioned above. Now no more than twenty thousand are alive.[70] A great number perished because of an illness they call viruela.[71] Many also died in wars [B3r], and a large portion died because of excessive work in the gold mines which the Christians forced them to undertake. This was against their custom, as they, by constitution, were a delicate people who worked little. In a very short time, such a multitude and large number was reduced into such a small number. Now, this island and all towns and cities on it are governed by a royal chamber and courtly tribunal based in the city of Santo Domingo, which they call Audiencia Real.

---

69. Federmann alluded to the *encomienda* system, in which natives were awarded to conquistadors as enslaved laborers.

70. We do not know how Federmann arrived at these numbers. Current estimates for the pre-1492 population of Hispaniola are about two hundred to three hundred thousand (Livi-Bacci, *Conquest,* 105). The native population decreased dramatically after 1492 to perhaps as few as five hundred by the 1540s (Rojas, Samson, and Hoogland, "Indo-Hispanic Dynamics," 21).

71. *Viroles* is the Spanish term for smallpox.

There I met Sebastian Rentz[72] of Ulm, the factor of the Welsers, my masters. I remained there for fifteen days and occupied myself with securing necessary provisions and with ship maintenance for my journey onward to Venezuela. I also loaded up ten horses there. Then I picked up and departed Santo Domingo, as mentioned before, in order to sail to Venezuela. It is 200 miles away from Santa Domingo even though the direct distance is no more than 150 miles. However, one cannot use the direct route because the ocean has too strong a current or flow.[73] If the ships do not take the higher route and want to travel directly, they are carried off course almost like by a fast-running river. We were traveling until the ninth day, which is a long time for such a short distance, because of the uncertainty of the route, as mentioned. On this journey, we did not find more than two winds that were favorable or useful. In the evening, around five o'clock,[74] an island came into view that is located seven miles from the territory of Venezuela, called Bonaire. The pilot or first mate of the ship believed it to be a different island, located seven miles above it, [B3v] called Curaçao. Misled by the pilot's or first mate's incorrect assumptions about this island, we traveled straight for the Venezuelan mainland[75] opposite from the island, incorrectly assuming that we would reach the port of Coro. This would have been the correct route or course if it had been the island of Curaçao, which we believed it to be.

Around midnight, one of the sailors noticed fires on three locations on the seashore near the ship that the Indio country people were burning in order to fish, as they customarily do. When the pilot or first mate of the ship detected this sight, he was startled because he was concerned that he had sailed too close to the shore. He recognized that the island we had seen before at night could not be the one we thought it to be. Otherwise, we could not have reached the coast of the land of Venezuela so quickly. Therefore, he hastily ordered the ship to turn around and to sail back until early in the morning

72. Sebastian Rentz was the Welser factor in Santo Domingo from 1529 to 1532.

73. Federmann refers to the Caribbean Current, a warm ocean current moving in a westerly direction between Hispaniola and the northern coast of South America.

74. Federmann repeatedly mentions clock time. He could have used a portable sundial or a novel portable clock or watch. A portable astrolabe, used for navigation, could have been useful too.

75. The term *Tierra Firme* commonly referred to the northern coast of South America.

so that they could see and recognize the land and their proper route, which was badly needed in our situation. If the Indios, as mentioned, had not lit the fires (perhaps owing God's providence) and we had not seen them, and if we had continued to sail for just half an hour longer, it would have been impossible for any one of us to get out alive. There was no port or safe approach in the area, only shallow places that were rocky just below the surface. The ship would have hit the rocks, and we all would have drowned.

After we had escaped this danger, thanks to said warning, as it was God's will, we saw land in the morning[76] and recognized that we had traveled to a point twenty-six miles away from the port of the city of Coro. There was no way we could reach the port of Coro from the place where we were because, as mentioned before, the ocean was flowing away almost like a river. [B4r] Furthermore, the winds there were most ordinarily or commonly blowing from the south or midday, making it impossible to sail toward the east or sunrise.[77] Out of two bad options, I chose the lesser evil. As I had to sail back to Santo Domingo, I resolved to avoid the great cost for so many people I had on my ship; I had 147 in my command. I would have incurred many expenses if I had taken them back with me. Therefore, I anchored the ship half a mile from land on the most secluded place that we could find on this coast or shore. In the evening, ten of us, all well-armed, jumped into a rowboat[78] (which is what the small boat is called with which one reaches the shore) and went ashore.

We settled down in a place we believed to be least visible to the Indios. We assumed that the Indios would arrive again at night for their customary fishing activities (as happened the previous night) so we could raid them and find out from them where in the territory we were. We also did not know if the Indios in this area were subjects of the governor of Coro and whether they were friends of the Christians. We could not expect anything during this night, however, because the Indios withdrew to safety in their villages when they spotted the ship. They were concerned that it was a pirate ship, as

76. The northern tip of the Paraguaná Peninsula.
77. This description makes sense only if Federmann had landed in Aruba, not Bonaire. From Bonaire, he could have easily sailed west to reach Coro with the help of the Caribbean Current, not east. In Aruba, they were much closer to the mainland than expected, namely the Paraguaná Peninsula.
78. "Batel," a small rowboat or ship's boat.

such ships often came from Santo Domingo, that had arrived there in order to round them up, capture them, and then sell them.[79] As I realized that our plan would not have its intended effect and result, we conferred with each other and sent two of our men to move inland [B4v] without being noticed. They were instructed to find and inspect a village or pueblo of the Indios and then return to report to us about the path there. This would allow us to travel there with the necessary strength and power and to be shown the way to Coro by them, through kindness or force. This is how the city is called where the governor and the Christians live and that they had built and constructed first. In case my men encountered one or two Indios they could overpower and seize, they should capture them and bring them to me so that I could find out from them what I needed to know through an interpreter I had with me.

The same night, after I had sent off the two Spaniards, I ordered all people who were not needed and necessary to operate the ship to go on land for three days, together with the horses and all necessary provisions, in order to prepare for the journey while waiting for the scouts. They reached a hamlet of three houses, five miles from where we had landed. They hid during the night, waiting for an Indio to move away from the houses so they could seize him and bring him back. However, this did not happen that night, but early in the morning, an Indio woman walked away from the houses alone in order to get water. They followed her. When they were about to snatch her, she talked to them in the Spanish language, which she knew a little because she had been sold in Santo Domingo years ago. She then was bought back by the factor[80] of His Imperial Majesty called Juan de Ampiés,[81] the first governor and owner of this land, and [C1r] returned to freedom in her fatherland. He did that in order to generate goodwill among the natives or Indios and to pull them closer to him. She asked why she was taken captive since she and the

79. Caquetíos from the coastal regions and from the islands of Aruba, Curaçao, and Bonaire were commonly enslaved and brought to Hispaniola to work in mines.

80. The term *factor* typically designated the manager of a foreign office of a merchant house, but it is used here for the administrator of royal assets.

81. Juan Martínez de Ampiés (d. 1533) was the founder of Santa Ana de Coro and the first governor of the Venezuela Province (1527–29), before the Welser Company took over its administration.

entire province called Paraguaná were friendly with the Christians in Coro. Thus they released her and followed her into her dwelling, where they found about sixteen Indios, men and women. Through said Indio woman, they informed and apprised the Indios why they were there, how we all had arrived there by ship, furthermore that we wanted to move on to Coro over land, and that we were seeking people to accompany us on the way. Thus the principal of the hamlet assigned two Indios to them. The two Christians returned with them in the morning of the third day.

After that I rose to travel to Coro with all my people. We reached a well on the same day, about two miles from where we had set out and where the ship was. We stayed there overnight. The following day, we reached said hamlet. There, the inhabitants waited for us with all kinds of fish, which were plentiful and tasty, and with other foods as well. They received us very well, and we stayed for the night. We sent several Indios toward Coro to the governor, who was not present in person; however, his deputy, called Luis Sarmiento,[82] was at home. Furthermore, we sent messengers to the villages through which we had to travel so they would be prepared with provisions.

Moving along, we arrived at a village called Miraca late at night the following day. We were well received, found what we needed, and rested until the following day. A number of my men [C1v] had overextended themselves the previous day because the distance traveled that day was six miles; we lacked water; and we mostly traveled in hot, sandy terrain along the ocean shoreline. Around noon, men arrived who had been sent by the governor's deputy in Coro to help us with our onward journey. As I assumed that my people were out of danger and essentially home, I gave the command to Georg Ehinger, who had traveled with me from Santo Domingo, with the order to personally turn over the men to the command of the governor or his deputy.

I turned around and began riding back to the ship. This was very important to me, as it was richly loaded and was anchored in a dangerous location. I rode back to the ship in one day and one night, a journey that had taken me three days before. On the fifteenth of January 1530, two hours past midnight, we raised the sails and

---

82. Luis Sarmiento served as acting governor from August 1529 to 18 April 1530.

traveled back so that we could take the correct course or direction and reach the port of Coro.[83] This port of the mentioned city of Coro was impossible for me to reach from the location in Paraguaná, where I had arrived. In six days we returned to the island Santo Domingo, as it pleased God. However, I did not want to return to the port, which is somewhat dangerous to enter, because I had no business in Santo Domingo. I ordered one man to get on land in the ship's boat or small boat at a port on the island called Azua[84] to where we had sailed, twenty-five miles from the city of Santo Domingo. He had orders to travel to Santo Domingo on land, to contact Sebastian Rentz, and to hand him my letters. [C2r] Sebastian Rentz came to me in a caravel to an island called Saona, where I had expected the man I had sent to him, but not Rentz himself. He brought to me all kinds of necessary provisions I had requested so that I could bring them to the [Venezuela] territory. I was anchored by this island for sixteen days in order to receive provisions and whatever else I needed as well as to wait for good wind and the right time to sail toward Coro again.

From this location mentioned above, I traveled to an island called San Juan,[85] fifty miles from the Isla Saona mentioned before. I traveled to a port and city that is inhabited by Christians, called San Germán. There I loaded horses, oxen, sheep, and other animals, as much as the reduction of the ship's weight allowed, which had resulted from me ordering my men to disembark and to walk to Coro. I was occupied with this for several days. Then I left to sail to the land of Venezuela again, along with another ship that also belonged to the Welsers, my masters, and that had joined me in San Germán. Thus we arrived in Coro, the proper port, happy and well on the eight day of March 1530, the almighty God be praised. It took me six months to travel from Sanlúcar de Barrameda, a port located in Spain, as told at the beginning, to reach the port of Coro in the land of Venezuela, that is, from the second day of October 1529 until the eighth day of March of the following year, 1530.

83. Coro is located about 5 km inland from its port (La Vela de Coro).
84. Azua de Compostela is a port city west of Santo Domingo.
85. The island of Puerto Rico, then named San Juan, after its capital.

[Chapter 2] How Nikolaus Federmann acted after his arrival in Coro in the absence of the Governor Ambrosius Dalfinger. Also with what reverence, splendid entry, and glory he, together with Hans Seissenhofer, received the returning governor mentioned above. [C2v]

Arrival in the City of Coro.

When I arrived in Coro, I did not meet the governor because he had begun a journey into the interior of the country eight months before.[86] Since his departure from Coro, there was no news from him. In the absence of the governor Ambrosius Dalfinger of Ulm, the land was governed by his deputy named Luis Sarmiento. I unloaded the ship with which I had arrived and prepared it for departure by the twenty-second day of March of the same year so it could sail back to Santo Domingo and onward to Spain.

On the eighteenth day of April, another armada of three ships arrived that was sent to Venezuela from Seville in Spain by the officials of the Welsers, my masters, so that their servants, one of them called Hans Seissenhofer,[87] could administer the land as governors. Those in Seville were concerned that Ambrosius Dalfinger had suffered a misfortune and that he and his people might have been prevented from returning by the Indios, particularly since there had been no news from him in such a long time, as mentioned before. [C3r] Furthermore, the deputy Dalfinger had left in charge, who was a Spaniard,[88] worked more for his own benefit than for that of the Welsers. Therefore, said Seissenhofer was accepted and sworn in as governor by the officials of His Imperial Majesty who reside and live in this country, like the *factor, contador,* and *tesorero*, these are administrator of assets, customs official, and treasury official, as well as by the other soldiers[89] and settlers. He then removed Ambrosius Dalfinger's deputy and gave me the command as deputy.

I remained and acted in that position until Hans Seissenhofer handed over the governorship again. About fifteen days after said

---

86. The first incursion by Ambrosius Dalfinger and 160 men to the area around the Lake Maracaibo took place from early August 1529 until 3 May 1530.

87. Johannes (Hans) Seissenhofer, aka Juan Alemán (d. 1532), was a Welser official who served as acting governor of Venezuela from 18 April to 3 May 1530.

88. The same Luis Sarmiento mentioned above.

89. Federmann uses the word "kriegßuolck" for this group. By contrast, he uses the term "volck" when referring to his men during the incursion.

Seissenhofer's arrival, the first governor, Ambrosius Dalfinger, returned. He had been absent for eight months, as he had undertaken a journey into the interior of the country, as said before, during which we were in fear and had doubts whether he would return. Half a mile from the city of Coro, he was received by Seissenhofer and myself under a pitched tent or field hut with a very splendid guard of honor of soldiers on horseback and on foot with trumpets and timpani, as well as with a sung mass and a *Te deum laudeamus*.[90] There we ate in the morning and then moved back into the city of Coro. Notwithstanding this Ambrosius Dalfinger, on said journey traveling through alien land unknown before, about one hundred Christians perished because of disease or military actions.

There would be much to write about the customs and ceremonies of their land, but I want to refrain from it because these are things I had only heard about but not experienced myself. [C3v] For it is not my intention to describe things other than what I saw myself and what I can recognize as truth from my own experience. Since Ambrosius Dalfinger had returned well, which we could not have anticipated for the reasons mentioned above, Hans Seissenhofer returned to the abovementioned Dalfinger, the first governor, his title of governor and captain general, which Seissenhofer had used by the authority of His Imperial Majesty until Dalfinger's arrival and return. He completely withdrew from the position and turned over to Dalfinger all soldiers and inhabitants who before had sworn allegiance to him and had subordinated themselves to him because of the doubtful return of Dalfinger. Against better advice, Seissenhofer wanted to free himself from governance after Dalfinger's return in order to more enduringly pursue different ventures in the Indies in which he had an interest.

Ambrosius Dalfinger, however, only made use of his governance until the last day of July of the year 1530. On that day, he prepared to travel to Santo Domingo in order to cure his illness of a fever recurring every four days, which he had brought home from his incursion, in addition to other good reasons he may have had. He could not expect relief in Venezuela while he remained in Coro. For this reason, I was sworn in again as deputy of the governor and captain general during his absence and was accepted in that position by all people.

90. "We praise you, O Lord."

[Chapter 3] The beginning of Nikolaus Federmann's journey from Coro inland, and what kind of organization and discipline he set up for his people on this journey. [C4r]
As I found myself in the city of Coro with too many people who were idle and without constraints, I decided to take a journey inland toward noon or the South Sea,[91] hoping to achieve something useful there. I prepared all the equipment that was needed for such a journey. On the twelfth day of September in the year 1530, I departed with 110 Spaniards on foot and 16 on horseback. I was also accompanied by one hundred native Indios from the land called the nation of the Caquetíos, who carried our food supplies and other goods that served our defense and sustenance.

On this first day, we traveled three miles away from the city of Coro and set up our camp in a meadow. I stayed there during the second and third day and created order among our people, which helped us travel onward in a quiet and orderly fashion. I also appointed subordinate officers and other officials, as the need arose. On the following day, we reached enemy territory, a nation called Jirajara, whose demeanor, manners, and customs will be described separately later.[92]

[Chapter 4] The Nation of the Jirajaras. [C4v] Of the nation Jirajara and their customs. Also how he was received with his people by the leaders of the land and by its inhabitants and honored with presents.
We soon reached and entered the first pueblo or village of this nation. They knew about our impending arrival, as I had announced to them through an interpreter, Cara Vanicero by name, as well as through several befriended Indios, that I intended to visit them to become friends with them. Thus we found the cacique, or leader of the village, with all of his inhabitants and subjects at home in a confident pose, with all the appropriate food and drink according to their custom. They also dedicated small, precious pieces of gold to us and received us altogether well. Nevertheless, there is not much gold in this nation nor on the land that they possess. They also have no mines, and neither do they negotiate and trade with neighboring nations because

---

91. "South Sea"—"Sudmöhr" in the text and *mar del sur* in Spanish—was a common term used to designate the Pacific Ocean. Also "mittäglich mör" or "Mittag mör," literally Midday Sea.

92. Federmann repeatedly promises more detailed descriptions of various Indigenous nations, which he never delivers.

each nation that lives in the mountains is hostile to the others. All eat human flesh, and each nation will eat a member of the other if they can detain or capture one of them.

Thus I traveled about thirty miles through the nation called Jirajara, which possesses a harsh and tall mountain range.[93] While traveling thirty miles through this nation, little happened [D1r] that is worth writing about, and there is no hardship to report. Our travel from one village to the next advanced without obvious problems since I was received well by this nation, although more out of fear than out of goodwill, and they only gave me provisions and some gold out of obligation. Furthermore, all of them submitted themselves to His Imperial Majesty and to me and my successors in His stead.[94] It is important to disclose with what difficulty and effort we traveled with our horses across the rugged mountains. Everybody can recognize how arduous and difficult it is to advance, particularly in places where no horse nor a Christian on foot has ever been, and what dangers await in many places while traveling through the high mountains, particularly where the inhabitants or natives put up resistance. Even though I had those villages observed where we were concerned about facing resistance before we entered the mountainous areas, we still could have suffered frequent losses if the inhabitants, as mentioned above, had been more adept or if God had abandoned us or not protected us out of His grace.

On the twenty-third day of September in the year 1530, we arrived in the last pueblo or village of this nation of the Jirajaras, which is called Hittova.[95] The inhabitants or natives of the village informed me how a two-day trip from here lived a different nation, who were their enemies, called Ayamanes. That is why the land between the two nations for the distance of a two-day journey is uninhabited and deserted. They also were a small people and dwarfs, yet valiant. They also possessed a rugged and mountainous land. I took along about 150 Indios or inhabitants [D1v] from the pueblo or village of Hittova so that they would make a path and trail for us. They also had to assist the other Indios we used in our supply train

93. Sierra de San Luis.
94. A reference to the *requerimiento*.
95. Location unknown; perhaps the modern city of Churuguara, north of the Río Tocuyo.

to transport our necessities and help carry provision and water in particular, which we would need on the way, as we were informed.

[Chapter 5] The Nation of the Ayamanes. Of this nation's nature, character, manners, and customs, and how they were liberated from fear, horror, and fright of the unfamiliar, never-before-seen, dressed, and bearded people and their horses through the friendliness and all sorts of presents from Nikolaus Federmann, etc., how they became subject to His Imperial Majesty, and how they gained and received a Christian name.

Early in the morning on the third day, we encountered six or eight houses in a desolate area, the first in the nation of the Ayamanes. The inhabitants were not aware of us when we raided them. They were frightened, as they had never before seen nor heard of horses and of dressed and bearded men. They tried to flee, which we prevented as much as possible. Through an interpreter, a native of the nation of the Jirajaras I had taken with me from Hittova, I had them advised and assured of anything that served peace, mollified them, and let them forget their terror. I also had them admonished about consequences, which was difficult for them to conceive and imagine. I also gave them several gifts of iron hoes and glass rosary beads, which for us (as we all know) are of little value but are highly regarded by them as foreign objects. [D2r] I stayed with them this day and demonstrated infinite friendship, hoping that this way I could make friends with the caciques or leaders of this land and nation. Through them I also investigated the setting of this land as well as its inhabitants and their power. Furthermore, I allowed the 150 Indios, who had traveled from Hittova with me, to return home, except for the interpreter. I also gave them presents and showed gratitude for the services they rendered so that the nation of the Ayamanes would be even more favorably disposed and could witness how we stood by our friends in good faith.

I departed from this desolate wasteland in the morning of the twenty-seventh day of the month of September in the thirtieth year, two hours before daybreak. Two miles from there, we reached a pueblo or village where a wealthy cacique or territorial lord allegedly lived. We wanted to raid him and befriend him like the others. The Indios from the wasteland mentioned before asked to be sent ahead to announce our arrival to the cacique or leader so he would not be shocked about our abrupt raid. I did not want to allow it because

I was concerned that they could leave their villages out of fear or inflict harm on us in a narrow passage if they became aware of our intentions.

When we got into view of the pueblo or village, the cacique or leader with his people appeared unconcerned about us, and we did not think anything other than that he would be there. I sent a number of men on horseback and on foot about a furlong[96] ahead, along with the Indios I had brought with me from the wasteland, [D2v] in order to talk to the cacique. If they could not make it happen amicably, they should forcibly stop as many inhabitants as possible. As soon as they would begin this, I would assist them. The only reason why I sent them ahead was that the inhabitants would have less fear and horror of a small number of people than if I had appeared with all my people.

However, when the scouts arrived in the pueblo or village, they did not encounter a single human being. We discovered that they had lain there during the night, as their fires were still burning. When I went there with all my people and confirmed what the envoys had reported, I got an inkling that the inhabitants had been warned by the Indios from the wasteland during the previous night while we slept. I could not let them notice that I wanted to punish them because I still needed them. We settled down in this village, as we found maize, yucca, sweet potato, and squash in abundance, the kind of provisions I will describe later.

We had been in this pueblo or village for two hours, while keeping good watch, and we deliberated how we could capture the natives or inhabitants. Then a group of Indios, whose number we estimated to be six hundred, came into view on a hill opposite from us, and they could be heard shouting loudly. They blew their horns, as they commonly do in war, and shot at us for a quarter hour. We could not stop them right away because they held the elevated position. [D3r] I did not want to give permission to shoot at them with arquebuses[97] since

---

96. While "furlong" is not an exact equivalent of the German "rosslauff," both are measures of length from the equestrian world, and both are equivalent to a Roman *stade* (stadium)—that is, about 185 m.

97. Federmann mentions "büxen," short for *Hakenbüchse* or *arquebus*, a long gun that appeared in Europe in the fifteenth century. This is the only time Federmann specifically mentions firearms.

we were able to evade their projectiles[98] because they were pretty far from us and had used up their munitions and supply of arrows. They robbed themselves of all without benefit to them. This was more useful than harmful to us because we used their ammunitions to arm and fortify the Indios in our supply train, which allowed us to force them to take the risky lead when approaching dangerous passages. I kept my men from shooting at the Indios because I thought that the damage we did or still were going to inflict on them would keep them from engaging in friendship with us later. While this would not have impeded our onward journey entirely, it would have made it more dangerous and arduous, at the very least.

I ordered an Indio, one of those from the wasteland, to talk to them and to let them know that we only had come to visit and to form friendship but not to take away their wives and children, as the Indios who wage war against each other customarily do. When they saw the Indio come toward them, they stopped shooting. After they heard him out, they left the hill with highly pitched shouts and disappeared on the other side, together with the Indio I had sent to them. Then they returned to us, one after the other. After that I ordered twenty well-equipped and armed men on foot to occupy the hill to observe the Indios and also to oversee the landscape. From them I learned that they saw about thirty [D3v] pueblos or villages that were located all around us. Three among them were on fire and burning, which the Indios had done themselves. Furthermore, they saw the Indios, who before had shot into our encampment, move away over a hill opposite from the hill where they had stood before. All these were not good signs to me. Since they had set fire to three villages, we had to assume that all had happened out of despair or distress and stubbornness because they were concerned that we would raid them. Rather than granting us enjoyment and sustenance, they burned all their goods that therefore would not be of use to them nor to us. I ordered this hill occupied and guarded for our security so that our base and encampment could not be attacked from any direction, particularly since our enemies could not be seen on the hill before.

Next I sent three Indios, who had come with me from the wasteland, to the caciques or leaders of the surrounding villages with

---

98. The generic German word "geschoss" refers to any object that can be thrown, fired, or shot at an enemy.

presents. Even though they were not in their pueblos or villages, they were easy to find and to catch, wherever they had their sojourn. Just as I had ordered the one mentioned before, I ordered the three men to inform the Indios why we had come there and to additionally relate to them that I would surely forgive their past misdeeds if they were to come to me and surrender amicably like friends. I would accept them as friends and also be their friend and furthermore help protect and secure them against their enemies. If, however, this was not the case and they would reject the friendship I offered, I would pursue them and also devastate and burn them, their land, and their cultivated fields. [D4r] I also would capture them and their wives and children and even hold and trade them as slaves and sold people. I would live and expose myself to them as a true declared enemy in every respect.[99]

After I had sent out the said Indios, a cacique with sixty men and women arrived at eight o'clock in the morning, entirely unarmed, as they customarily do when they yield as friends. Even though this cacique or leader was not a small person like the dwarfs we encountered, as will be told of later, he nevertheless brought some dwarfs with him, some among them measuring five or six spans[100] at most.[101] I had this cacique or leader baptized, along with the people he brought along, and had them instructed about the Christian faith, as much as could be inculcated.[102] For why is it necessary to preach to them for a long time and to lose time with them? With God's blessings, these things have to be instilled over time in the young, who do not know yet about the seductive and demonic ceremonies and cults of their fathers, and not in the old people, who are obstinate.[103] To

99. Federmann described the logic of the *requerimiento* with its promise of benevolence in the case of submission and threat of violence in the case of resistance.

100. The term "Spanne" (span) indicates the distance between the tip of the thumb to the tip of the little finger, generally around 20 cm.

101. Here, the editor or printer added the first of only a handful of marginal notes: "Dwarfs five and six spans tall."

102. The baptism mentioned here implies the presence of clergy who are otherwise not mentioned, with the exception of a monk [O4v]. All incursions under Spanish jurisdiction had to be accompanied by a member of the clergy.

103. This is Federmann's only subtle critique of the required conversion ritual. His insistence that faith has to be instilled over time implies a Lutheran viewpoint. Federmann's impatience also indicates that his focus was not on establishing durable institutions, in contrast to the intentions of the Spaniards.

this leader, I gave a few small, precious ornaments of gold, of the kind they like to wear as adornment, that had been given to me in reverence, in addition to several knives and scissors. I affirmed peace with him, as he, along with all his people, submitted himself in obedience to His Imperial Majesty, on whose behalf I was there, and to myself. Through him I also notified all surrounding Indio principals or leaders that they should come to me, like him, and surrender as subjects of His Imperial Majesty and as our friends. This allowed me to spare villages when I was moving through the land, [D4v] depending on whether their inhabitants were friends or enemies.

During the following five days, during which I remained in the pueblo or village, many caciques or leaders from many pueblos or villages arrived. I administered baptisms and admonishments to them, also intended as a warning, as I had done with the cacique or leader mentioned before. Even though these were all members of the nation of the Ayamanes and were dwarfs, I nevertheless found many among them to be of a larger disposition, or length and size of body, both men and women. When I asked about the reasons for this difference and discrepancy, I was told and informed by them that many years ago, a great and general or common dying occurred in the nation of the Ayamanes, which their fathers still remembered. At the time, they lived in the land without being mixed with other nations or people. This illness is called viruela, like what we call smallpox, for in all of the Indies, there never was pestilence before.[104] Such a large number or multitude of the Ayamanes or dwarfs died from it that there were not enough of them anymore to keep their enemies from occupying their land. Out of necessity, they allied themselves with a number of villages and intermarried with their inhabitants of their enemies, the Jirajaras, who were located next to them toward midnight. As a result, a number of people with a larger disposition and better stature, that is, with a longer and larger body, were raised among them in this place. Yet they reported to me that the land a four-day journey inland from this village was inhabited exclusively by dwarfs and very small people, who were intermixed with no other nation.

---

104. European disease sometimes arrived in Indigenous communities before the Spaniards did.

[E1r] After I had asked them about that and had found out from them what was necessary to continue my journey, I set out to advance to the said dwarfs. I was accompanied by many Indios from village to village who served us well by making a path and meeting other needs. Through them I made friends with many villages and caciques or leaders along the way, and I did not need to use force against them. When they saw how other nations that were related to them surrendered and how I kept my promises to them, they loyally provided everything we needed.

I set up camp next to a river called Río Tocuyo on the first day of October of the thirtieth year, where we arrived late in the day. This river runs very fast in a valley and also is wide and deep. We made a raft with bucklers or shields, which the men on foot use for their defense, cover, and protection, and with several trees that we cut down for this purpose. On it we ferried across our belongings, along with the Christians who could not swim. We pulled the raft from one side or riverbank to the other with a rope, for the rapid and mighty flow of the river would have carried it away otherwise. After we had set our people across the river in the described manner, with great effort and risk, and had gotten the horses to swim across, the night settled in, and we set up camp right at the edge of the water, not worried about a threat from the water. Around midnight the water of the river had risen very high because it had rained in the mountains, as we presumed, although there were no storms where we were. It had risen [E1v] as high as two men higher than in the evening when we had crossed it. It flowed around the elevation on which we rested so that we were surrounded like on an island. It carried away several of my people who were lying in the lower areas, along with their equipment, clothing, and food supplies, before they became aware of the arrival of the flood waters. Furthermore, two horses were swept away a quarter mile downriver from our encampment. Our best remedy or response was to hang all belongings on trees, the best we could, and to take advantage of the elevation, as we could not leave it.

Had God directed the water to rise for three more hours, it would have inflicted serious damage on us, and there is no doubt that nobody would have gotten away who had not climbed a tree. As it pleased God, may He be praised, the flooding lasted barely five hours, and it dropped as fast and quickly as it had risen. In the morning, before noon, the water was as low as before, and the swollen river

that had surrounded us had run off. For this reason we were forced to
stay there for the day to search for the lost equipment even though
our food supplies started to run low. We found the two horses and a
few of the possessions that had gotten stuck in the shrubs and trees.

We continued our journey the following day, that was the third
day of October in the thirtieth year. We arrived in a pueblo or village
where I was well received by the inhabitants, who were also the
enemies of the Ayamanes, because I had sent ahead of me the Indios
I had taken along with me from the villages mentioned above who
belonged to the nation we had befriended. [E2r] I received needed
provisions from them as well as good advice. I remained there all
day until early the next morning. At eight o'clock I rose up to travel
toward the mountains of the Ayamanes. To be sure, the cacique or
leader and the inhabitants of this village are enemies of the dwarfs
in the mountains. Here the land began where the dwarfs live by
themselves without being intermixed with other nations, as indicated
before, and they tolerate no Jirajaras among themselves. Furthermore, they are not in a confederation or alliance with the other
pueblos of their nation, who are also Ayamanes but who are mixed
with their neighbors, the Jirajaras, nor do they have anything in common with them. Even with the pueblos who are intermixed with the
Jirajaras through marriage, they are hostile and hateful, as indicated
before.

After I had traveled a mile, we came to a desolate mountain range
too strenuous and dangerous for the horses. As we considered the
mountain range ahead of us to be very rugged and jagged, I arrived
at the following conclusion. Even though we already had begun
to make a passage or path, we would encounter the same situation
every half mile. Our journey would slow down considerably, and
the dwarfs would become aware of us and either inflict harm on us
from the mountains or leave their villages and move away. When
we would reach their villages, we would not find them there, and we
would have traveled in vain for they surely would have hidden in the
mountains. Thus we would not encounter them, or perhaps we would
do so in places that were more dangerous and risky for us than for
them. We could not hope to be received by them like we had been
[E2v] by the Indios of this nation we had encountered earlier because
they did not know us nor had they heard of us. More likely they
would see us as enemies, as the ones who supported those they hated

and opposed and who came to do them harm. I had only chosen this route to see this nation because I was curious about their smallness, according to hearsay. This did not serve our planned journey, namely to move on to the South or Midday Sea. This mountain range made it impossible to travel forward at this moment, as the horses would have hindered us more than they would have helped us overcome the enemies.

Therefore, I sent a captain with fifty of the best-armed men on foot, along with an interpreter of this nation, so they would bring the dwarfs to me with kindness and friendship, or with force if that was not possible. I withdrew with the rest of my people and stayed in the pueblo or village where I had left on the same day, as told before. There I waited until the next day, which was the fifth day of October, for those I had sent out. They arrived late in the evening and brought around 150 persons, men and women, whom they had raided in a village five miles from the village where my encampment was. When they resisted and did not want to visit[105] me and come to me voluntarily, they were captured. Many of them were killed in a skirmish, and several Christians were injured by them as well. When the Christians and their prisoners were returning and were on the way back to us, a large number of them followed in order to extort the captives. [E3r] From the hills and mountains that they always occupy, as is the custom of the land, they harmed and wounded many of the Christians, as well as many of the captives who were divided up among the Christians.

All of them were small people, and among them, no other nation was mixed in, as predicted by the Indios mentioned before. The tallest measured five spans, but there were some among them who only measured four spans. Yet their bodies were of an appropriate proportion and built to match their height. Unfortunately, we could not use these people because of their small size, even though we would have badly needed them as we had a shortage of people in our supply train who could carry the belongings of the Christians. The reason was that most of the Indios we had brought from Coro had escaped and had returned back home. I had them baptized and had them

---

105. In the phrase "freiwillig mich haimzůsůchen," the verb "heimsuchen" refers to a visit in one's own home, implying that Federmann viewed the village as his domain.

instructed and reminded to keep peace, like the others before. Thus I put them on the right path, and I also connected and befriended them with the cacique or leader of the village where we had our camp, whose enemies they had been. I let them return home, with the exception of ten people who accepted me as their leader the most, and I ordered them to praise the good deeds they had experienced from me to their cacique or leader and to bring him several presents and gifts that I had them take along. In addition, they also should tell him that they all should come to the village of Carohana,[106] which is located three miles from there, to visit with me and to confirm their peace with me. I planned to travel there on the same day in order to wait for them until the following day. Thus they went on their way in peace as freed captives, and I went on mine.

In the pueblo or village of Carohana, I found good accommodations and friendship because they had friendly relations and a confederation and alliance with the cacique or leader [E3v] of the pueblo or village from where we had just come. We stayed from this day to the next, which was the seventh day of October. There we found plentiful and excellent venison from deer and stags of which there is an abundance everywhere.[107] Around noon, two caciques or leaders of the dwarves arrived with a lot of their people who were fully armed, which they do not ordinarily do when they plan to be friends or to surrender. The inhabitants of the pueblo or village of Carohana were cultivating their fields when they detected the dwarves from afar, before our guards had become aware of them. A turmoil arose, and a crowd gathered because they were worried that the dwarfs had arrived in order to raid them as their enemies. I asked why they gathered, also fully armed, as I was unsure if this was directed against us. The cacique or leader of this village had me informed that his enemies had come to raid him, asking me to offer him protection and help. When they came closer to the pueblo or village, the interpreters told me that they were the caciques and leaders of the pueblos or villages of the captives I had released the previous day. The moment they noticed us, they lifted their bows up in the air in one hand, which among them is a signal for peace.

106. Likely the modern city of Carora.
107. Brocket deer and white-tailed deer are native to Venezuela.

After I ordered them to sit down, about three hundred of them, I reprimanded them because they arrived fully armed, violating the norms of friendly conduct. I would have raided and defeated them if the interpreters and fellow members of their nation, [E4r] the ten I had kept and not released, as mentioned before, had not held me back. They offered the excuse that they had to come fully armed because of their enemies and that they needed their arms in order to return home safely. They also presented to me many presents or gifts of gold in reverence. Furthermore, the cacique or leader presented or gifted to me a dwarf woman who measured four spans and was of a very good and beautiful proportion and shape, and who he said was his wife. Such is the custom among them to confirm peace. I welcomed her even though she reacted badly and cried violently because she believed that she was gifted not to humans but to devils, whom she thought us to be.[108] I took this dwarf woman along all the way to Coro, but she remained there because I did not want to take her out of her country because she and all other Indios would not survive long outside of their fatherland, particularly in cold lands.

I united this cacique or leader with the inhabitants of the village where we stayed, whose enemies they had been before, as mentioned before. They also subjected themselves to the obedience of His Imperial Majesty and successors. Nevertheless, I refrained from demanding tributes or services expected of subjects as long as I was not better armed and did not have a stronger force than they did. Furthermore, the subjugation of this and of all other nations of the Indios under the authority of His Imperial Majesty as well as their display of friendship only last for as long as they cannot think of something better to do.

I traveled another five days through this nation. [E4v] Everywhere I was received well by the Indios or natives because I sent ahead the Indios whom I had turned into friends, from one village to the next in order to announce our arrival in the pueblo or village we were approaching. I also had them informed that we treated this nation in good faith and that we had not come there to inflict harm on them without cause. We received few presents or gifts of gold in this nation because they have no wealth and own very little. For their

---

108. Here a marginal note: "The Christians were not regarded as humans by the Indios, rather as devils."

adornment, they only used these black glittering kernels that feel like rosary beads when touched. They also make use of some shellfish or sea shells that they buy from other nations. These shells are alien to them because they live far from the ocean and therefore know nothing about the ocean and never get near it. They are a people who are enemies with the surrounding nations, their neighbors. They also do not travel far and do not violate the borders and the territories of the others.

On the twelfth day of October, we reached the last pueblo or village of the nation of the Ayamanes or of the dwarfs. After that begins a different nation of the Gayones, who are also enemies with the Ayamanes mentioned above. Therefore, we first had to procure, obtain, and acquire a friendship with benevolence and also without it.

[Chapter 6] The Nation of the Gayones. [F1r] How these Gayones were raided and turned into friends with presents. Who later absconded with the cacique or leader and congregated for an uprising and resistance. Who were raided a second time at night and taken away as prisoners with force, and their leader put into iron chains for breaking the peace. Also how inconstancy and distrust were avenged and repaid.

Next I resolved to establish order with the Gayones like I had done with the other nations before, as already mentioned. Without warning, I raided them in a pueblo or village early in the morning before daybreak. Even though they offered resistance initially, they were subdued. Through the Ayamanes, of whom I had several with me, I had them apprised and informed about the reasons why we had come there. At this point they seemed satisfied and gave me several presents and gifts of gold as well as all needed provisions. Thus we settled into several houses at a location that was most convenient and advantageous for us, believing that we would stay there for one, two, or three days and turn the surrounding Indios and pueblos or villages of this nation into friends, like others before. This would ensure that we could travel forward more smoothly and also with less danger.

I ordered the Ayamanes who had come with me to return to their boundaries and borders, safely accompanied by some Christians of my people, because they were concerned that they would be attacked by the Gayones, their enemies. Even though I had the intention of creating friendship between them, [F1v] the Ayamanes did not want to allow it. They stated that a number of their fellow Ayamanes had been captured or slain by the Gayones but had not yet been avenged. I did not care much about that, as my only objective was that they would have fewer doubts about our just friendship and also would recognize that we were there for their well-being. Other than that, we easily could have tolerated them being enemies of each other, as we would have had to be less concerned about them forming an alliance, which could have been harmful to us.

Since I had pacified this pueblo or village and also its inhabitants, I believed that we were given the presents or gifts as pledges of friendship and that we were kept in good faith by them, as we were by other pueblos or villages. However, the cacique or leader, with all his people, women and children, absconded or disappeared secretly at night and left us alone in their deserted pueblo or village. We only became aware of this in the morning because they had withdrawn into the houses furthest away from us. We thought that they had done this to remove their wives and children from our conversation or dealings. As we had to assume that their unexpected escape or flight served nothing other than a hostile assemblage of their friends in the surrounding villages, I ordered the hills around us, from where we could expect to be harmed most, to be brought under our control and to be occupied by Christians.

I remained there until the evening. At about five o'clock, I sent out approximately fifty Christians, four among them on horseback, and also four Indios from our supply train. Those Indios serve well as advance guards in such raids. [F2r] Along with them I sent an interpreter from the nation of the Ayamanes who was traveling with me and knew the nature of the country well. I ordered them to raid the nearest pueblo or village, which was close according to the interpreter, and to capture as many of them as they could. I ordered them to do so in the night at about three hours before daybreak, at a time when one pays least attention to enemies and when everybody is asleep, which is what happened. They assaulted a village that was located about two miles from our encampment. There they captured about eighty persons, men and women; the others had escaped. However, they returned with the captives around eleven o'clock, close to midnight. They did not see the need to follow my order, namely to only attack close to daybreak, because this was a small village with few people that was easy to control without that added advantage.

I interrogated the captives regarding the whereabouts of the cacique or leader who had fled from me from the pueblo or village. Right
away, during the same night, I sent another fifty men, with a number
of the captives, who had to show my men the way to the hideout, in
order to assault them. When the Christians approached them, clearly
at the right time when one usually sleeps, they found them keeping
good watch. So the Christians took away their breath and put out the
lights of their fires, which they habitually light at such times when
they are in fear, and attacked them with a lot of shouting to make
it sound like there were many of them. The Indios got frightened,
yet set up a defense, wounded seven Christians, and shot dead one
of them. The other Christians buried him in a secret place where
nobody would come so that the Indios would not notice[109] [F2v] and
find out that we were subject to death, for they thought us to be
immortal. Many Indios died, and forty-three of them were captured,
among them also the cacique or leader. I had him forged in chains,
along with others I brought along in iron chains, because he broke his
pledge in spite of his assurances.

I divided up the remaining captives from the two places among
my people in order to carry their equipment and belongings. We had
a great need for them, as many of the Indios we had brought along
had escaped. We wanted to relieve those we still had of the load they
had carried for a long time and of their drudgery in order not to
wear them out completely and to conserve them for emergencies. For
instance, they could help us fend off enemies in dangerous passages
where they could move about easily and without raising suspicions.
Even though they would be seen, from a distance they would be
thought of as local country people rather than enemies and thus
could be useful and serve us well. We could trust them as staying
with us, and our squad offered their only hope to return to their
fatherland through so many alien nations.

Thus we traveled for five days, just to write about this briefly.
During this time we could not turn a single village into friends
even though I often sent ahead one of our captives with presents
in order to encourage the native caciques or leaders of a number of
villages to engage in friendship. I also ordered the scouts to convey

109. Here a marginal note: "The Christians are considered to be immortal by the
Indios."

the reasons why we had apprehended the previous captives. This did not work out, however, because neither the scouts nor the villagers returned. Hence we found deserted and empty all the pueblos or villages through which we moved, as our arrival had been announced to all these nations by the companions of our captured Indios who had escaped. [F3r] Therefore, we never saw any Indios in this nation. Only twice, in two narrow passages, a number of them shot into our encampment from a hill where we could not harm or overrun them. They inflicted little damage with their arrows. Yet, they easily could have gotten rid of us had they waged war with rocks that they could have thrown at us without effort. However, God the Lord did not let it happen and endowed them with a lack of skill and spirit.

[Chapter 7] The Nation of the Achagua. How this nation and people, fearing a quick raid by Nikolaus Federmann and his people, who they believed to be more devils than humans, surrendered in obedience and friendship, and how they proved and showed this sufficiently (albeit forcibly) with the favor of presents of gold and offerings of all necessary provisions and other supplies.

As we arrived at the last frontiers and villages of the aforementioned nation, another nation began, called the Achagua. Until the fourth day, we traveled in the middle of a river that runs in a valley between two mountains since the Gayones do not use a different path to get to this nation. When I queried the prisoners, they responded that this was the case only because these nations were each other's enemies. Also both parties eat *Carne humana*, that is, human [F3v] flesh, and they go after each other with all the ruses they can think of. They make their way through the water as naked people who are generally more fish than flesh in their nature. They do this, except for when the water has risen very high, so that their movements cannot be traced or detected, for both nations never live quietly and unconcerned about their enemies.

Although the Indios walk only a day and a half until they leave the trail in the water, it took us four days, as mentioned before, because it was troublesome to get through with the horses and all our belongings. During this time, we never got out of the water except for at noon and in the evening when we found a small flat area along the banks of the river where we could sit down to eat or rest at night. We also had more shortages in provisions than abundance, as we had counted on reaching the villages earlier, based on the information from the Indios who were our captives. Once we reached the path on land and were able to leave the water, we were facing no less of a struggle, namely turning the inhabitants of the nation of the Achagua into friends. We had no means of making peace with them because the aforementioned neighboring nation was our enemy, and we remained without alliance or association with them. Therefore, we did not have the opportunity to corroborate the reasons for our journey and to verify that we were not there to injure them. However, it was to our advantage that they were enemies with the aforementioned Gayones and that they therefore were less distressed about the harm and imprisonment the Gayones had suffered through us.

When we approached the first village of this nation [F4r] that was still three miles away, according to the Indios from the Gayones, we settled down. We guarded all positions and surrounding hills so that we would not be seen by the Indios or inhabitants, which would have caused an uproar among them. I also sent out a large portion of our men at night in order to raid them and to bring to me whoever they could capture. This happened indeed, and they returned in the morning, before noon, with a few people they had raided while sleeping in said fairly small village. The villagers did not mount a defense because they were horrified about the unexpected attack by these unknown people they believed to be more devils than humans. I would have liked to have the means to offer them peace and concord and also to make them forget the heavy heart and the damage they suffered so that they would not remain enemies like the Gayones. This was quite worrisome, and furthermore, this made it very burdensome and arduous to secure food supplies and provisions as well as to learn about the nature of the country.

Moreover, I did not have an interpreter who could serve and advance this objective and whom I could trust. For the only two I had with me were from the nation of the Gayones, as described before, whom we brought with us as prisoners and who also spoke the language of the Achagua. As much as we would have liked to avoid this, there was no other option. I ordered the one interpreter I considered to be more suitable to be informed that I wanted him to be free and unrestrained and that I wanted to have him escorted through the country of the enemies up to the boundaries or borders of his nation. I also wanted to give him presents with the condition that he brought the nation of the Achagua to peace with plain language that is not deceitful and with the words [F4v] that were dictated to him by me. He also had to tell them that they had caused their banishment with their own actions because they had left their villages and fled and banded together against their own promise and pledge. This he promised and set out to do.

Then I released five of the Achagua who had been captured first, but I retained most principals and nobles, including the cacique or leader, so that they would be less likely to resist us and instead would obey us in order to gain freedom for their leaders through means other than war. To the released captives, I gave presents that cost very little for us but are highly valued by them. They should bring those gifts to the caciques and leaders of the surrounding villages, announce and signal to them peace and leadership on my part, and inform them that we came solely to obtain their friendship and to protect them against their enemies. Furthermore, they should tell their leaders to come visit me to confirm peace with me in the pueblo or village called Coary,[110] where they had been captured and to where I was just about to leave.

When we arrived there on the twenty-fifth day of October around nine o'clock in the morning, several caciques or leaders arrived during the same hour as well. With them came, by four o'clock in the evening, about eight hundred people, men and women, who all lived about two or three miles away from there. In their hands, they carried sticks that could not be used as arms, of the kind they customarily use to attest to their friendship. They also brought me presents of gold, along with all necessary provisions and venison. I remained in place in this [G1r] pueblo or village for two days. During this time, I was visited by the caciques or leaders of many surrounding villages.

I have to write only briefly about this nation and its land through which we traveled in five days, while maintaining good friendship and loyalty. We encountered nothing during those days that is worth writing about in particular or mentioning specifically. On the last day of the noted month of October, we arrived in a pueblo or village called Cacaridi, which is the last village of this nation. We calculated the distance from Coro, the city where we first had left at the beginning of our journey, to be seventy-three miles. I can probably

110. Location unknown.

write that I encountered the roughest mountain range I have ever experienced. We were in locations where there never had been horses before. It was difficult for us to get through with our horses because of many mountain passes and especially to get through the nation of the Gayones, who had remained our enemies, as mentioned before. Therefore, we were deprived of their help building trails, and the Christians had to do it themselves even though we had close to 250 Indios, men and women. They carried our food supplies and other goods, such as munitions that would serve us later for our defense. We needed them badly, as they lightened the load for the Christians. We would not have been able to advance without them. Had this lasted longer, it would have demanded a taxing effort and intolerable labor.

However, the mountains ended three miles from this pueblo or village, as will follow, and the most level and most beautiful land opened up that can be seen in the Indies, which is owned by the nation or people of the Caquetíos. We were quite surprised [G1v] and had a hard time believing it when we heard of it from the nation of the Achagua. We did not believe it, thinking that they did not have the same language and did not speak the same way as the Indios in Coro, from where we had set out, even if they were also called Caquetíos. As mentioned before, we had traveled seventy-three miles from there and through five nations, each of which spoke a different language. This was such a thing that was more entertaining to us, as it usually happens, the more incredible it is.

You surely have to consider how doggedly we had to strive to communicate with each other until we reached the Caquetíos. Only for the first language, that of the Caquetíos, I had two Christians and trusted interpreters with me who knew that language very well. After that, with the Jirajaras, I had to speak through two, with the Ayamanes through three, with the Gayones through four, and with the Achagua through five people. Until the first understood the next and then conveyed up to the fifth language what I had ordered him, each of them no doubt added or subtracted something, so that among ten words I had ordered to the first, there was hardly one word spoken to my liking and addressing our needs. By no means did I consider this to be just a small or minor hardship, as I sensed that this hindered our investigation of the secrets of the country, which often forced us to move on.

The aforementioned nations or people, namely the Jirajaras, Ayamanes, Gayones, and Achagua, all eat human flesh,[111] and each nation
is the other's enemy. Later, I will report on each of the nations, their
manners and customs, as much as I have learned.

**[Chapter 8] The Nation of the Caquetíos. [G2r] This nation is populous
and very combative, and it also has an abundance of gold. Using their own
power, they forced all neighboring nations to move from the plains into the
harsh mountains so that they own and inhabit the most beautiful, most
level, and most fertile land. When the Christians arrived (who desired the
friendship of the Caquetíos), they turned out to be hospitable, dedicating a
substantial amount of gold[112] without coercion (solely out of curiosity to see
these unknown people, the Christians).**

When we departed from the last pueblo of the nation of the Achagua, as mentioned before, we advanced to within a mile of the
Caquetíos who inhabit the flat land. They were described to us by the
Achagua as populous and very belligerent. We already had reached
their villages that are located in a very beautiful plain, as indicated
before, along a great river, and we could see about twenty of them.
There we settled down and deliberated how we should handle this
situation. From there we saw many pueblos or villages from where
a large number of native Indios, who wanted to reject our friendship, could inflict damage on us, and we were concerned that they
would offer resistance to our detriment. We had learned about the
strength, audacity, and agility of this nation of the Caquetíos from
the Caquetíos who live near Coro. We carried that knowledge with us
in addition to what the Achagua had indicated to us, as I mentioned
before. Furthermore, all other aforementioned nations were forced
by them to live in the mountains so that they alone could possess
and rule the flat and most fertile land. [G2v] These Caquetíos did not
inhabit mountains in any location, neither around Coro nor in this
area. Instead, they only inhabited the best, most fertile, and most
level land and did not tolerate other nations in any plains.

After appraising our security needs fully and adequately, we
arrived at the decision not to raid them like we had done to the other

111. Here the marginal note: "Four nations, eaters of human flesh."
112. The word "gelt" is used here by the editor, which could refer to money but
also other compensation. The chapter later refers to gold.

nations because there were too many of them, and in all seriousness, we had little to gain from this. Instead, we decided to send a Caquetío Indio, who had traveled with us from Coro, together with some Achagua, who peacefully contracted and traded salt from the last pueblo of their nation with the Caquetíos, in whose land and villages we wanted to travel. We sent them to the inhabitants of those villages and pueblos in the province or region called Barquisimeto with many presents for the caciques or leaders in order to inform them of our arrival and about the purpose of our journey. We also instructed our envoys to tell them that they should move toward us and make peace with me if they were willing to be our friends.

While we did not count on making peace quickly and amicably with this nation, we nevertheless considered setting things up in the way described here as the safest path forward because we could first assess their mood before relinquishing our advantage. Therefore, we stayed put at said place about a mile from their pueblos or villages all day and the following night, with a good guard and defense. Since it was quite late when we sent out the Indios, they did not return with a response during the same night. This had the advantage for us that we could make use of our horses that were our best defense. The Indios were most afraid of them [G3r] and suffered great harm from them.

Early in the morning, those we had sent out returned with many Caquetío Indios but not more than forty of them. They brought venison and other foodstuffs with them. They notified me that their caciques or leaders were awaiting us in their pueblos or villages, that they gladly wanted to retain us as friends, and that they anticipated our arrival with joy and pleasure. I sent them back home with the message that I wanted to follow shortly. Even though they offered to wait for us and to show us the way or just to travel with us, I kindly turned them down so that I could gain critical information in their absence from our envoys about the intentions and dissimulations of these Caquetíos, which subsequently took place.

I could not find out anything other than we did not have to be concerned about deception or animosity on their part, owing to the Caquetío or interpreter whom I had taken along with me from Coro, as mentioned above, and had sent to these Caquetíos. He highly praised our fair conduct and good behavior, according to his own statement, which we demonstrated to all nations who submitted to us in friendship and proved through deeds and gifts. He also related that we had displayed our power and strength against those who had resisted us. In response, they agreed to be our friends and to give to us whatever we needed. This is why I gave him a present and freed him. Up to this time, he had served a Christian as a present from me.

After he had informed me about the large size of the villages and the large number of people, I could appreciate that they mostly wanted to have a look at us as a people they had never heard about before, [G3v] aside from the speech by this abovementioned Indio and interpreter that may have moved them as well. Because of their large number and strength, they perhaps were also confident that they would be able to offer valiant resistance in case we wanted to deal with them with force. This insight allowed me to conclude that they would have regarded moving toward us as humiliating, as other nations discussed before had done, and would have considered it dishonorable to follow our commands and orders because of the perception that they would have obeyed out of fear.

When I reached the first pueblo or village of this Barquisimeto province, I found a large number of Indios, about four thousand in number. They were a very well-proportioned and strong people, and I was received very well by them. To make this short, I stayed for fourteen days in these pueblos or villages that are located along this river in order to inspect all the villages and to turn all the inhabitants into friends. There were twenty-three of them, and they were all half a mile but no more than one mile apart. I also learned about the parts of the land we had to travel through on our planned route. They demonstrated good friendship to us in all respects, and in these pueblos or villages of this Barquisimeto province, they gave us presents of 3,000 pesos[113] in gold, which is equivalent to 5,000 Rhenish guilders,[114] as a form of unsolicited and voluntary veneration. For they are a wealthy people, who process and trade a lot of gold, and one acquires and buys it from them. One can obtain much gold and great wealth in return for gifts of iron, such as hoes, axes, knives, and the like, [G4r] of which they are very much in need. This is important to

---

113. The gold weight of a peso was 4.18 g. We can assume that Federmann received approximately 12.5 kg of gold.

114. The Rhenish guilder (lat. *florenus Rheni*) was the most important gold currency in Germany at the time. The standard fine gold content at the time was 2.527 g.

consider, as they gave us so many presents and gifts out of good will, solely to demonstrate their own magnificence, and not out of fear, as other villages and nations we had traveled through before had done.

We could sense that they had little fear of us because they could be confident in their large number, as mentioned before. I definitely believe that about thirty thousand proficient and skilled Indio warriors could be assembled out of the twenty-three villages within half a day, as I will show later when I describe their manners. In addition, they inhabit and own strong and well-fortified villages that could not be raided like the pueblos or villages we had seen before. This is because they are enemies with the four nations that surround them on all four sides. Therefore, they have to be concerned about and prepared for war and assault by their enemies and have to engage in it occasionally against their adversaries, like the three nations that surround them as well as several villages of the Achagua, whose enemies they are as well. Even though they are allied with several of the nearest villages of the Achagua and swap and trade with them, for example, some trade salt to them, the Achagua also are their enemies, as stated above.

Furthermore, they have the nation of the Ciparicotos on the other side, and on the third side, they have the nation of the Cuibas. All these three nations eat human flesh, and they also butcher and slaughter their enemies that they capture in war or however else.[115] On the fourth side, [G4v] they have enemies in their own nation of the Caquetíos in the populous valley, that is, in the inhabited and densely populated valley called Vararida,[116] which will be discussed later when we travel through here again while returning to Coro. We suspected that they settled and lived so close together so that they could withstand their enemies more attentively and effectively, because they have to deal with so many enemies. On our journey so far, as well as later, they are the most populous or largest people we had encountered in a such a small area, so close together, and with such good defenses and strong villages.

In this province, I found news about a different ocean, called the South or Midday Sea, which was exactly what we so eagerly had

---

115. Here a marginal note: "Three nations butcher and eat each other."
116. The valley of the Río Turbio, the upper reaches of the Río Cojedes, around Barquisimeto. A district of Barquisimeto is called Bararida today.

hoped to reach, since reaching this ocean was the main reason for our journey, as mentioned at the beginning. There we could likely hope to find great wealth of gold, pearls, and gemstones. Similarly, these were found in abundance in other jurisdictions in the Indian countries that bordered the South Sea. Even though the inhabitants of these pueblos or villages talked about this, none of them claimed to have been there. Rather, they asserted that they only had heard this from their elders. We sensed that this was an excuse so we would not expect or force them to accompany us there.

In those fourteen days during which I stayed there to visit and inspect the villages of this province, as indicated before, about sixty Christians became sick, [H1r] and many among them could not be moved from there, neither on horseback nor on foot. Even though it would have been necessary to stay there longer to wait for the sick to return to health, the Spaniards attributed the cause for their ailment to the unhealthy air and humidity of this province and hoped to get rid of their illness by moving away from this place and this air. Therefore, I departed the next day in order to move toward the ocean that was indicated to us. I had many of the sick carried in hammocks.[117] This is what the Indian beds are called, which I will explain later. I used the Indios in our supply train for this purpose. I made the inhabitants understand that the sick men were carried because they were great lords. Others had to ride on horseback. The healthy ones and those who owned the horses were on foot, while the sick ones sat up on the horses one behind the other. We dissimulated against the Indios as much as possible so that they did not realize that we Christians, whom they thought to be immortal, also were subject to diseases. Had they noticed, this would have brought us quite a few disadvantages, and they no doubt would have been encouraged to wage war against us.

You have to consider at what an inconvenient time they would have attacked us and in what a desperate situation I was. I did not see a feasible path that would have allowed me to either travel back or move forward with sick and defenseless people in a vast and unknown country. I found myself among a people on whose friendship I could rely only as long as I had control over them and as long as they believed themselves to be too weak to resist us. Furthermore,

---

117. "Hamacos."

we did not know what nations were ahead of us and whether they were enemies of the Barquisimeto province. [H1v] We had to assume that this was a well-defended people because they could endure and withstand hostile actions from these villages that had the strongest buildings and people. However, all this could not keep me from traveling forward and taking the planned itinerary because we had nothing good to expect from traveling back and waiting for the sick to return to health in the nation of the Achagua. This would have been regarded as fearfulness and timidity by the natives or Indios and would have diminished our reputation or credibility, as well as the fear they had of us, which would have caused them to rise against us. Choosing the lesser of two evils, I went on my way in the manner described above, more like gypsies and cripples than as soldiers.

We were given two hundred Indios by these pueblos or villages to carry our belongings and also to show us the way to within view of the villages of their enemies, which was a different nation called the Cuibas. I assured them that I would accompany their men back into their custody from the land of their enemies. As you heard before, our carriers were mostly needed to carry our sick. We asked these Indios who carried our belongings to walk in front, and we did not pay attention to them and also were not worried about them betraying us. We simply thought that they hurried ahead of us because they were loaded so heavily and so they would be able to set down the load they were carrying. However, they carried our belongings no more than two miles, left everything behind in the field along the path where we would come through, and escaped. Perhaps they were concerned that we would bring them into the land of their enemies, [H2r] force them to serve us further, and thus would not honor our commitments.

Now we did not have enough people to carry our belongings. We had no choice other than dividing them up among the Christians. As there were few healthy ones and as these would be loaded down first and therefore would have become tired, we would not have been able to offer resistance to the enemies who would have attacked us. We therefore picked the most necessary items out of our luggage and distributed them among the Christians. The rest I had buried in a secluded place until we returned because we no longer had the means to carry it forward. As mentioned before, the Indios who were supposed to show us the way had escaped. Luckily, a small boy and an Indio woman, who were not able to follow the Indios who had left us, remained among and with the Christians. The Indio woman spoke the language of the Cuibas a little, but she did not want to admit that she knew the way.

[Chapter 9] The Nation of the Cuibas. In what danger the Christians, after suffering hunger for a long time, reached the first village of this nation that uses poisoned arrows against their enemies, attacked it to their advantage, and won a hard-fought victory in battle against them. How they were forced to run up to a second village, where the inhabitants were hiding out of fear of the prior battle, locked themselves into a house, left precious pieces of gold and also food items outside on the path, believing that they could please and divert us. As they could not force the Christians to withdraw, they were finally persuaded to engage in friendship and submission, which caused the entire nation to become obedient.

[H2v] We traveled between two mountains in a valley with a great river called Coaheri[118] as far as we could until the evening of the same day. We could not see any villages or settlements of the Indios. We were a little anxious and worried about the lack of food because we did not have any provisions, as we had nobody who could carry them for us. Therefore, we sent out two men on horseback early the next morning, each to a separate location in the mountains. Each should ride to the top of a mountain to look out for smoke and people in the countryside so that we could get there right away and would not again fail to attain provisions the next day, which would have left us without strength and would have made it nearly impossible to move backward or forward.

The scouts returned soon and with encouraging news. One of them had seen a great plain from the mountain as well as the end of the same mountain range. It would not be more than a mile to get out of the valley into the plain. While he had seen neither villages nor smoke, there was hope that they would not be far from there. It was impossible that such good and level land through which such a great river was flowing, along which we had traveled through the valley, would be uninhabited or deserted. When we reached the plain, I moved to an elevation with my people from where I could observe both the plain and the men I was going to send out. Thus I dispatched

---

118. Likely the Río Cojedes.

two each on horseback, in four different directions. Their task was
to follow the paths for an hour or two, until they had found some
pueblos or villages and cultivated fields, and then to brief us since we
had no less a shortage of food than an abundance of hunger.

[H3r] While I stayed on the elevation and waited for the scouts,
we saw smoke rise in many places in the surrounding mountains.
We understood that we had been discovered by the inhabitants. The
smoke from these fires served to pass along a battle cry and warning from one village to the next. Even though we had to be worried
about them banding together, we were pleased to know where their
dwellings were. Now we could raid them and alleviate our lack of
food in case our scouts did not find cultivated fields with provisions
for us, since our need for food surpassed our fear of the enemies.
Many of my people had become very defiant, as if they had been led
astray. Moreover, there was no shortage of people who fantasized, as
commonly happens, that the Indios who had fled from us, as mentioned before, had left us for the lone reason that they perhaps knew
that the land was not inhabited and that they had slipped away from
us because they did not want to suffer hunger with us. Some even
claimed that the Indios had escaped from us on purpose to drag us
into famine and even death. However, all this stopped when we discovered the smoke from the fire, which indicated that people indeed
lived there. I did not leave unpunished those who spread such ideas
among our people, in addition to faintheartedness and rebellious
conceits. Had the relief or help been delayed only by one day, I would
have had reason to be concerned about a considerable danger from
my own comrades, who were supposed to obey me as their commander and to perform their duties.

Not long after that, two of the scouts returned who had seen and
witnessed a number of houses and several grain fields nearby but had
found the village deserted and uninhabited. [H3v] We moved toward
the houses and set up camp there. There were only six houses located
in a beautiful plain close to a creek, from where we could look far
over the land. Even though the grain on the surrounding fields was
before its time, it was more than ripe to us at this time of need. The
hunger gave it a better taste, as did the thirst to the fresh water, as if
it had been the best wine and partridges at a time of abundance.

The same evening, I sent out a captain with thirty men on foot
to raid one of the villages, where we had seen smoke during the day,

and to bring me as many inhabitants as they could capture in order to make peace with them, as had happened with others before. When the scouts got close to one of the pueblos or villages at night, they saw and observed its inhabitants keeping up good watch and defense next to their fires of the kind they customarily light in times of war. They did not consider their own numbers adequate to assault the villagers and therefore returned without achieving anything, asking me to release more men. I decided not to do this because we had many sick men. I did not have enough people to raid said pueblo or village while leaving a sufficient number with the sick ones for their protection. The village was located in the mountains, in an area where horses could neither be useful nor accomplish anything. For that reason, we were not strong enough to assault the natives or Indios and their pueblo or village because we would not have had the benefit of the horses. At locations where horses are useable, one man on horseback [H4r] can achieve more and also is feared more than fifty on foot.

I was not in a hurry to move on because in this place where I had settled down, I had a good and safe encampment. This was probably the tenant farm[119] of a cacique or leader in the area, as there were only six houses that, as I thought, were only used and inhabited at a time when the surrounding crops were harvested. The land around it was level, and we would have been able to see our enemies from far away if they had wanted to assault us. In addition, we also could have used our horses there, which gave us our most important defense, courage, and support. Furthermore, we were not lacking water and maize, which is their grain, nor venison from deer, which we needed daily in our encampment. There are plenty of deer, and they do not run away quickly because these animals are not made skittish by the Indios, who have neither horses nor dogs, and for this reason, they can be stabbed easily by men on horseback.

After we had rested there for five days, we thought that our sick would revive and recover to some degree. However, this was not the case. Therefore, I sent out ten men on horseback and thirty-five on foot. They had to search the plain, along the water, to see if there was a single pueblo or village that was in such a location where they

---

119. Federmann called it a "meyerhoff," a term German audiences could relate to. A *Meierhof* was part of a large noble or ecclesiastical agricultural estate that was occupied by a local administrator.

could overpower the inhabitants. If they could not be convinced to
come to me amicably, they could be brought to me forcibly by cap-
turing as many of them as possible. If at all possible, however, they
should be spared so they would not suffer great harm and not many
of their people would be killed, as this would make it even harder or
impossible to commit them to friendship.

[H4v] On the same day, my men reached a pueblo or village about
three miles from the place where I had set up camp. There, a large
number of Indios were preparing for their defense and resistance.
When two men on horseback came within range of a crossbow shot[120]
of this village in order to inspect it and consider their options, they
found the village surrounded by trenches. They realized that it was
impossible to enter the pueblo or village because they would not have
been able to overcome the inclines and trenches without suffering
harm. Therefore, the captain ordered the men on horseback not to
approach. Only those on foot went with him so that the inhabitants
could see only the first two horses who had inspected and spied on
the pueblo or village, as said before. The other eight horses were
hiding behind a grain field that was so tall that a man on horseback
could not be seen. When the Christians approached, preserving
their advantage as much as they could, the captain made a backward fleeing motion. This emboldened the enemies to abandon their
advantageous position in order to pursue those who were apparently
fleeing. There were about five hundred of them. They were held up
by the men on horseback who were hiding in the grain field and then
attacked from behind and from the front by those who had appeared
to be fleeing. In the battle, about sixty of them were captured, forty-
eight stabbed to death, and the others put to flight. Among the
Christians, only four were injured but not mortally, and also a horse
was shot. This was the first pueblo or village where we encountered
poisoned arrows, about which I will report later.

Of the prisoners who were brought back to me [J1r], I released six.
I gave presents to them that they had to bring to their leaders. I also
instructed them, as I had done with other nations before, to say and
relate to them whatever furthered peace. They also should get their
caciques or leaders to come to me so I could return to them their

---

120. The range of crossbows at the time was at least 300 m, perhaps shorter for
smaller, portable types used in the field.

prisoners, two of them being leaders or nobles. One of them was seriously wounded; I had him bandaged and well treated and cared for.

By the third day after I had released the abovementioned Indios, nobody had arrived, which we could not attribute either to good or bad intentions on their part. Many of us were of the opinion or belief that the surrounding Indios were assembling in order to assault us and to pry the prisoners from us with force. Others opined that this was happening out of fear instilled in them because of the harm they had suffered and that they did not dare to come because they were worried that we would capture them as well and not keep our pledge, even though they would be coming to redeem the prisoners and pay homage[121] to us as friends. Besides, we had nobody they could trust who could confirm to them how we customarily treated those who surrendered to us.

Early in the morning on the third day, I sent another two Indios, in the same manner, to bring the caciques or leaders to me. They should point out to them how well they were treated and cared for by us even though they were captives. I had this communicated to them by the Indio woman I had brought along from the Barquisimeto province, who, however, was not abundantly proficient in the language of the Cuibas. Yet we had to make do with her even though it hampered us more than a little, partly because [J1v] of the language in which she was not proficient, as mentioned before, and partly because she was a woman who was not endowed with the courage that was necessary to tell them what we had instructed her with a confident spirit. She also had a fear of those who are disagreeable and hostile to her own nation.

After I had released and sent out these Indios as well, I was riding out on the same morning with twelve men on foot and eight on horses for a hunt and set out to pursue deer. We came very close to the pueblo or village from where the prisoners were. We were in view of a multitude and large number of Indios, with women and children, some armed and some unarmed, on an elevation located above the village. Sometimes they allowed themselves to be seen, and sometimes they were hiding behind a small hill so that we did not know how to assess this situation. Since women and children were among

---

121. Federmann used the German verb "huldigen," referring to a formal act of submission and recognition of the legitimacy of the ruler.

them as well, we could establish that this was not a war assembly. Rather, we believed that the village people rose in order to leave the pueblo or village and to perhaps resettle in the mountains in a remote area where they could not be found.

I hastily sent for the said Indio woman in the encampment who was our interpreter with them. When she was brought here, it was about three o'clock in the afternoon. We decided to approach the pueblo or village, close enough so that we could hear each other speak. I instructed the interpreter to call out the inhabitants. However, those in the pueblo or village did not respond so that we believed that they had left the village unoccupied and deserted. Subsequently we rode into the village with great caution and with a rear guard. I placed a number of men in a spot from where they could observe the elevation on which we had seen the Indios before [J2r] and could warn us if they wanted to take action against us.

However, we did not see anyone in this pueblo or village until we got close to the center of the village. In front of a large *bohío*[122] (this is how their houses are called), we found a number of precious pieces of gold displayed on two chairs, along with several pots with food and venison, but we did not see or find anyone there. However, when the Indio woman, our interpreter, attempted to open the door to the bohío or house, as she had done with other houses before, she found it secured and locked but heard people in there. I instructed them, through her, to get out, pay homage to me, and close friendship with me, as I had come here for this reason alone and not to inflict harm on them. They did not want to discuss this any further and answered from within that we should take the gold and the other goods in front of the door and send their prisoners back to them. In response, I had them told that I was not here because of the gold, as I had plenty of it myself, and that I had sent them presents of a higher value. If they were to come out of the house voluntarily, they would experience and suffer no harm. If they did not do this, however, I would order the house, in which they were locked up, to be set on fire and burned down. The poor people were not concerned about this because they believed themselves to be safe, as if they were locked into a fortress. Finally, they opened the door. Their leader or most noble

---

122. Federmann uses the word "Buhio," from the Spanish *bohío*, based on Taíno *bohi* and Arawak *bohy*. This term typically refers to a large house of a cacique.

person came out first, then all the others one after the other. There were about a hundred of them, a strong and joyous people, but also well-defended.

I had the question addressed to them what their intention was [J2v] when they considered putting up resistance against me, given that I was powerful enough to devastate them, even an entire army of theirs, with a single horse I was sending against them, notwithstanding the fact that I had a lot of horses. As many among us carried deer we had caught behind ourselves on our horses, I let the Indios know how foolish they were to think that they could resist us since even a deer with all its speed was not able to escape us. Furthermore, the skirmish with them would ensue solely because of the anger of the horses, which we would not be able to control entirely because of the disobedience of the Indios. Therefore, we would have to give in to the horses, and we would have to allow them to have their way with the Indios. My intention was not to inflict harm on them but rather to negotiate with them peacefully. If I had bad intentions against them, I would be powerful enough to eradicate all of them and to allow none of them to get away. I was just blustering splendidly in order to instill fear in them, but I also wanted to impress on them that we had friendly intentions with them.

They apologized right away. Since they did not recognize us nor knew anything about us, they were setting up defenses against us, as they expected nothing from us other than what enemies usually do. But now, after they had heard otherwise from my emissaries about why we were here, they were on their way to visit us and to surrender to us. They were prevented from doing so during the previous few days because they had to bury their dead who had been strangled or killed by us. When they now saw us approach from afar, they were concerned that we had come to wage war on them. [J3r] This is why they had sent their women and children into the mountains and locked themselves in to be safe against the first assault, until we were able to hear their intentions peaceably, namely that they wanted to surrender to us as our friends. They also gave me gold that I found, as said before, lying on the chairs in front of the bohío or house, and that I refused to take at first so that they would not think that we had arrived because we desired to pile up a lot of gold.

Then I sent out some of them with the order to bring back their women and children into their villages and their peaceful dwellings

where they had lived before so that I would not have to doubt their
genuine friendship. I took the others with me and returned to them
their relatives who were our prisoners and also gave them presents,
like knives and rosary beads, that they held in high esteem. Furthermore, I ordered them to summon their friends from the surrounding
villages of their nation to come to me and to confirm their friendship
with me as well.

During the following nine days, during which I was staying in the
village where I had originally settled down, many of the surrounding caciques or leaders arrived to visit me and also to bring presents
to me, and I treated them as friends. The delay at this location,
which was required to pacify this nation and to learn more about the
manners and might of its inhabitants and whatever else was necessary for us to learn, was quite useful for the safety of our journey
forward.

We erroneously expected the sick to return to health. We did
not consider their ailments, such as fever or open wounds that were
caused by the water, [J3v] to be of any consequence. Yet we faced
more illness than health during these days when we were resting. For
such illness was not the fault of the humid Barquisimeto province,
as we had believed, but solely of the four days of hardship and travel
through the water and additionally of the unfamiliar liquids and food
that was unripe at the time. Indeed, we were lacking the food that
would have helped an ailing human return to health.

Therefore, I soon moved away from this village for the sake of our
sick people, with much effort and labor, as we had done in Barquisimeto, in order to reach the other ocean that was not far from the
nation of the Cuibas, as they assured me. They told me that it was
closer than it is in actuality so they could get rid of us. It is important to remember that we were not welcome guests no matter how
peacefully we lived there. Therefore, we traveled slowly for five days
with the sick and with quite a lot of baggage, two, three, or up to
four miles each day at most, moving from village to village. Nevertheless, we got assistance from Indios who helped carry our supplies
and belongings and other necessary items. They also announced our
arrival so the inhabitants of the villages did not shun us and persuaded them to be our friends.

On the fifteenth day of December in the year 1530, we reached
a large pueblo or village called Acarigua that also belongs to this

nation. It is located next to a great river[123] that is at least as wide as two crossbow shots. The shore of the river was populated or inhabited for the distance of a quarter mile. [J4r] Even though a large number of the houses were located closer to the plain and looked like they were similarly built to those in nearby villages, unlike the others, all of them nevertheless had only one leader and the single name Acarigua. There, around sixteen thousand Indio warriors live, as we estimated, not counting women, children, and old people who could not serve in a war. These inhabitants were in part Caquetíos and in part Cuibas, who lived amongst each other. I was received well by them, as I had them notified before of our arrival by the Cuibas who were their friends and ours and through whose land we were moving. They demonstrated good friendship to us by offering a number of presents of gold and also venison and a range of necessary foods.

Nevertheless, I sensed that it was not advisable to remain in this village for too long. We felt somewhat outmatched by the large number of inhabitants, particularly with so many sick people. Furthermore, they have an abundance of poisoned arrows, which they use more frequently than the villages we had experienced before. At the same time, we had few means to continue our journey, as the many sick people prevented that. So we stayed there, from day to day, willing to be vigilant, until the fifteenth day. We were sustained with an abundance of fish, venison, and other foods to take care of our needs, which helped us greatly to rest and to await the improvement of our sick. Since the pueblo or village was large and there were many inhabitants, we were less burdensome to them.

During that period, two of my Christians died, and a few of the sick recovered or improved, which would have advanced our journey. During this period of fifteen days, [J4v] I sent out a captain with thirty men on foot and five on horseback toward several pueblos or villages of a nation called Coyones, whose enemy they are, who live at the foot of a mountain four miles from Acarigua, the pueblo or village where I had settled down. I did so following the request of the inhabitants and because I was inclined to appease them so that they would doubt our righteous, truthful friendship even less and would lodge fewer grievances. About eight hundred of the inhabitants accompanied them with a captain of their nation, who was told to

123. Presumably the Río Acarigua.

obey and follow the orders of the captain appointed by me regarding
attacks on enemies.

Those who do not know the disposition of this nation might
consider it a bad move to deprive myself of so many people. If the
Indios really had intended to separate us this way and to attack and
defeat us while we were not united, we would have had little hope
of prevailing. For in both groups, there were few of ours, and many
sick ones stayed behind in the village with me. However, all of this
was carefully considered by us. It is important to know that the fear
the inhabitants have of horses, as mentioned frequently before, is
so great that I could expect to be able to fight back with ten men on
horseback and a few on foot, on level ground where horses are of
help, against a much larger number than I can or want to write about.
I do not want to be perceived as writing this to glorify myself and
those who were with me. For almighty God has to act in our favor or
interest against the infidels, otherwise I would have to be silent about
this journey, [K1r] and otherwise it would have been impossible for
such a large number of natives to be overcome by so few Christians,
such as Hernán Cortés in Yucatán,[124] also Pedro Arias Dávila in Nicaragua,[125] Hernando Colón as the first discoverer and explorer of the
Indies in Santo Domingo,[126] and furthermore other imperial governors and captains in the Indian countries. Each of them, by themselves, could not have prevailed against the masses of the enemies
and Indian peoples. This is impossible to believe for those who have
not seen or experienced it.[127]

Those who want to know about these things should read what
Hieronymus Seitz and others have translated from the Spanish language into our German language[128] and also read from the accounts

124. Hernán Cortés (1485–1547) and his men subjugated the Aztec Empire in 1519
to 1521. The area was sometimes referred to as Yucatán at the time,

125. Pedro Arias Dávila (1468–1531) served as governor in Panama and Nicaragua
in the 1520s.

126. Hernando Colón (1488–1539), the second son of Christopher Columbus
(1451–1506), was a bibliographer, book collector, cosmographer, and his father's biogra-
pher, which may explain Federmann's obvious error.

127. Federmann here confidently presents himself as a peer of Columbus, Cortés,
and Dávila. Federmann was aware of their reports but also heard about these men in
Santo Domingo, where all of them had lived.

128. The Augsburg merchant houses collected travel reports and had some of them
translated into German by Hieronymus Seitz and others, but never published.

or reports that have to be submitted separately by each commander, in which each has to be accountable for his actions.[129] There the evidence for what I said or indicated as well as for many other miraculous things is presented and shown to be well-founded truth, which is what I am doing here as well.

Getting back to our previous topic and undertaking, the added benefit horses offered to us, as said before, was the reason why we took over a road right next to the water in the village of Acarigua. We protected it with good guards day and night, and I ordered that two men should ride up and down the pueblo or village at every hour of the day to check whether they could discover any changes among the inhabitants. If they had intentions to attack us, we would be able to notice beforehand because they could not pull it off as long as they did not move away their women and children. For they had the attitude that they only wanted to tolerate little and minor harm to their own people. [K1v] Even thought they would have been able to kill and overcome all of us, they were not prepared to do so in order to avoid the perceived detriments. As they know how to do everything *a su salva*,[130] that is, to their advantage and without any danger to them, this also is the way they engage in battle.[131] Even if they suffer few casualties, and among ten thousand, only two hundred or three hundred perish, their troops scatter, in particular if they lose their head and leader. If victory or triumph is already achieved and no other man loses his life, they remain as determined and steady as we are, and nothing could be gained from them. They conduct war only from afar, from as far away as they can shoot, and do not come near each other. This is why they often said to us that we do not know how to wage war because we run close to the men right away and confuse them, which causes them to become disheartened, as they are not used to this. This is enough to prove that with so few Christians, such a large number of Indios can be dominated and overcome, for the benefit of those who out of ignorance doubted the matters discussed above and more pertinent things that happened and occurred to the abovementioned commanders in the Indies.

---

129. Federmann's use of "Relationen" is a reference to the *relación de méritos* or *probanza de mérito*.

130. Presumably "a su salvación," "for their salvation."

131. Here a marginal note: "Customs and attributes of the Indio warriors in their wars and battles."

During the time when I sent the abovementioned Christians to
their enemies, called the Coyones, I had the cacique or leader, the
highest commander of the pueblo or village of Acarigua, live with
me in my dwelling, day and night. I did not let him out of my sight,
as I was very certain that his subjects would not dare to undertake
anything against us without him, as long as they knew that their
leader was not with them but rather in our hands. This was the best
pawn for our security. However, I assured the cacique or leader [K2r]
that this is happening in his honor and out of friendship and that I
was granting him the stay in my dwelling so that he could see that
I did not intend to undertake anything against him. He had to show
that he believed that, whether it was in his heart or not. I conversed
and talked with him about the exploration of the land and in particular of the South Sea, about which we had received news before,
as already mentioned. They also reported to me about two ways to
travel there.

**[Chapter 10] The Nation of the Coyones. How the first village of this nation
that was raided by the Christians showed a strong and serious defense,
from which the Christians suffered injury. After they did not want to
accept the offered peace and friendship, nor wanted to hear about it, the
Christians, against their intentions, were forced to act against the Coyones
as serious and hostile enemies by burning their houses and engaging in
a bloody battle, in order to avoid harm and humiliation for themselves.
As a consequence, six hundred of them were captured, but their nation
remained undefeated so that the Christians had to accept a different path
to continue their planned journey.**

When the envoys to the Coyones returned on the third day, that was
on the eighteenth day of December in the year 1530, they brought
with them about six hundred Indios from a pueblo or village they
had raided at daybreak. They had orders from me to bring as many
as possible [K2v] to me unharmed and not to treat them as enemies.
Likewise, the Christians were to prevent the Caquetíos and Cuibas
Indios from doing this, of whom eight hundred from the pueblo or
village of Acarigua went along, as mentioned before. Even though
I had promised otherwise to the inhabitants of Acarigua in order to
pacify them, it was not my intention to offend the Coyones. Rather, I
wanted to turn them into friends of ours and of this pueblo or village
and to end their hostility. The reason for this is that one path that

was indicated to me as leading to the South Sea went through the nation of the Coyones. This is why I would have liked to see them kept as friends.

When the Christians, together with the Indios, were approaching this first village, only the Christians attacked while the Indios formed the rear guard. This was because we did not trust them to move against the Coyones, their enemies, without a bloody attack, which was unnecessary and also ran against my order and the underlying objectives. However, when the Christians assaulted the first street and the houses along it, the Indios barricaded themselves into their houses and inflicted harm on our men out of there so that ours could not get close to them in order not to be harmed and thus could not inflict harm on them. The Indios did not respond to all admonishments and requests to establish friendship or to attempts to talk about why my men had come there. The Indios did not want to hear our thoughts, nor did they cease shooting. Thus the last remedy or solution was to set the pueblo or village on fire so that all the Indios would have to come out of the pueblo or village and also leave their houses or burn to death. Thus our men captured around [K3r] six hundred persons, as described before, men and women along with their children. Many of them burned to death even though some of them could have escaped, yet many of them rather burned to death voluntarily than fall into the hands of their enemies. Two of the Christians were shot to death and about fifteen wounded. Furthermore, a horse got shot that died eight days later as well. Many of those Indios who were our friends were injured as well.

I took little pleasure in this foray, both because of the harm my people suffered and because of the annihilation of our enemies, which of course could not be undone with remorse. Furthermore, the envoys, as you heard before, were forced to do all of this because they could not return without having achieved anything. This was not advisable because it would have been interpreted as timidity by the Caquetíos and Cuibas, our friends in the pueblo or village of Acari-gua. This would have greatly diminished our status and would have caused them to be less fearful of us, much to our disadvantage.

Subsequently, I gave about two hundred captives to the cacique or leader and to a number of leaders or nobles of the village, mostly children or very old people, also some who had burns and could not serve us. I gifted them as slaves or sold servants in order to compensate them for the harm their people had suffered and to firm up our friendship.

On the third day of January of the year 1531, I set out to travel through the nation of the Cuibas toward the South Sea, where we believed it to be at the time based on the legends and assertions by the natives or inhabitants. [K3v] The path through the land of the Coyones was restricted and blocked because they remained our enemies even though it would have been a little closer and less swampy for the horses, according to our information. While the number of sick people had decreased little, the captives from the Coyones who had reinforced our supply train by four hundred offered great relief and help to us.

On the same day, we arrived in a pueblo or village called Tohibara,[132] whose inhabitants showed us good friendship that had been procured and acquired before by the people from Acarigua, whose friends they are. There we learned that in order to continue or complete our journey, we had large and deep swamps ahead of us, and we were concerned that we could not get through with our horses. The inhabitants apprised us that in three days we would reach a pueblo or village from where one could see the said South Sea. Therefore, I sent five men on horseback and twenty-five on foot to travel to this village or pueblo called Itabana[133] to find out if they could get there in a different way without obstacles and without threats from enemies. They should not risk being away for more than six days, three to get there and as many to return, so that we would not be separated too long.

On the third day they reached a great river[134] that separates this nation from another nation or people called Guaiqueríes. There the land of our friends ends. They could not cross without great danger because those on horseback and those on foot would have had to swim across and thus would have lost their advantage. Furthermore, from there to Itabana [K4r] was as far as they already had traveled, all of which, we were told, was only a three-day journey. Therefore, they returned, as they were ordered not to stay away longer, leaving behind as friends the pueblos or villages through which they

132. This town and location are unknown today.
133. Likely near the modern town of El Baúl.
134. Likely the Río Cojedes.

had traveled up to said river. My men also learned from the Indios that other people who wore clothes, who also were bearded,[135] and who were like us in every respect, as they described it, supposedly were operating and trading in Itabana, the village that was said to be close to the South Sea. They allegedly had arrived in a large house on the same body of water, which they told us was the ocean. We were unsure whether these were Sebastian Cabot's[136] people who had settled or explored a town with the same name along the Río de Solis[137] three years ago. There Cabot had found a great body of water on which he had traveled inland for three hundred miles[138] on a ship that the Indios translate as house. The jurisdiction and rule of this Cabot adjoins the jurisdiction and rule of the country of Venezuela in a southerly direction.[139]

This news instilled us with confidence that we could reach the Christians. This was a big relief for us because we could learn from them about the other ocean and about circumstances and secrets of the land and its inhabitants. Furthermore, if they intruded into our jurisdiction, we could keep them from doing so.[140] Or we could save them if they suffered distress and had been tossed there because of bad winds, which would have answered a great need of ours as well as theirs since we needed to increase our numbers.

[K4v] After I learned this news, I moved on from Tohibara straight toward said river on the twenty-third day of January of the same year. In two pueblos or villages, called Curahy and Cazaradadi,[141] I encountered peaceful inhabitants who awaited us with presents.

135. Reports generally noted that the natives did not have beards nor were able to grow them. Federmann's assumption, therefore, was that these bearded people were Europeans.

136. Sebastiano Caboto (ca. 1474–ca. 1557), the son of John Cabot, explored the Río de la Plata region from 1526 to 1530. Federmann was unaware that Cabot was back in Seville at this point in time.

137. The Río de la Plata initially was named after Juan Díaz de Solís, who explored it from 1515 to 1516.

138. Federmann probably referred to Cabot's journey on the La Plata and Paraná rivers. Three hundred Spanish miles roughly correspond to the navigational distance to Asunción.

139. The distance between Asunción and Federmann's location in Venezuela was over 3,000 km.

140. As colonial territories initially were defined by coastlines, conflicts between conquistadors about territories in the interior of the continent were quite common.

141. Neither village can be identified today.

However, from the village of Cazaradadi onward, I found all villages to the abovementioned river depopulated and deserted. While my scouts had reached it in three days, I needed five days with my sick men. Furthermore, the inhabitants of that village were hiding and had fled even though they had remained friends with my scouts. We believed that they did that out of fear. Perhaps they surmised that the scouts had only been there to explore the land and that I had come to assault them.

When I reached a village called Curahamara,[142] located two miles from the river, I found nobody there either. This was inopportune for us, as we now had nobody through whom we could close friendship with the nation of the Guaiqueríes, which we were approaching. For that reason, I was forced to stay in that village, to look for the inhabitants, and to follow them around. This is what happened, and I sent people to two different places. When they discovered the cacique or leader with many of his people due to a fire they had lit in a remote forest at night, my people assaulted him, captured him along with about eighteen of his people, and brought them to me. While censuring them because of their escape, I told them that the reason why I had them followed [L1r] was because they violated the commitment they had made to my people. I untied him and his people and also honored him with several presents. Then I took them along to the nation of the Guaiqueríes, whose friends they are.

[Chapter 11] The Nation of the Guaiqueríes. Of the coal-black, proud, brash, and evil people of this nation, what aggressiveness, defiance, and faithlessness they proved to the Christians, who also attacked them traitorously, which, however, turned into a great disadvantage for them. How the cacique or leader was captured and shot to death after a long interrogation under torture (in order to find out about his betrayal and secret assault on the Christians) and how after that five hundred of the assembled people were slain. Furthermore, how a cacique of a different village was kept a captive forged in chains (because of his deception) and led away with others. Also how the Christians were betrayed cunningly by a third cacique who got away with his people because of it.

When I arrived at the said river called Coaheri, I encountered about six hundred Indios of the Guaiqueríes on the other side, a people

---

142. Town and location are unknown today.

who are coal black; there will be more on their customs later. I had the cacique or leader of that nation come to me whose villages are a mile and a half from the river. They only have their fishing houses by this river and also hold their markets there. For the nation of the Caquetíos, who live both on the other side and on this side, buy fish from them in return for fruit and other food items, as the Guaiqueríes only engage in fishing and rule the water.[143] These two nations live mixed among each other and live in peace, yet each by itself, in separate [L1v] pueblos or villages, which is why each nation needs the other. From this river onward, all the way to Itabana, we found the most stubborn, wicked, and deceptive people that we had encountered so far on our journey.

When the cacique I had sent for arrived, he appeared with many of his people, who were fully armed, resembling black devils more than human beings. I reprimanded him because he did not arrive with friendly gestures, how friends customarily do. In addition, I ordered him to be instructed and told that he should notify me what his intentions were so that I could take appropriate measures. I also behaved toward him as if I had little interest in being friends with them, although this is not how I felt and also did not address our needs. Thereupon he let me know quite confidently that he came armed because of the lions and tigers[144] of which there were many and of whom he allegedly was scared. He added that we were carrying our arms as well, and yet we were praising ourselves that we were coming here for the sake of peace. Even though he made himself heard in excess and with too much pride, I had to endure it this time and dissimulate with him. However, he had to pay dearly for that, as will be shown later.

I told him that I wanted to travel to Itabana to visit some of our associates who were there and that I wanted to leave behind most of my people in the pueblo or village of Curahamara. I ordered him to supply them with fish for their sustenance. He retorted that the fish belonged to his subjects, each owning as many as he fishes, but that the fish would not be denied to my people [L2r] for compensation or payment. Then he recommended that I take all my people with

---

143. Here a marginal note: "Guaiqueríes coal-black fishermen."

144. There are no lions and tigers in the New World. Federmann refers to cougars (mountain lions) and jaguars, both native to Venezuela.

me because the people of Itabana were good warriors against whom
I would need all my people. Supposedly, they had slain a number of
the people we called our associates who had arrived there in a house.
Thus they confirmed or corroborated and endorsed what I had heard
about the Christians from other Indios, as mentioned before. I let
him know, however, that I had no shortage of people I wanted to take
with me. For as many as there were of them in Itabana, I wanted
to advance with far fewer of my people, and those I took with me
mostly had the duty of assisting me. It was not the intent of this
cacique or leader to issue this warning for our benefit. Rather, he was
concerned that we were too close to him, that he would have to sus-
tain us with fish, which I would demand of him, and that he would
have to endure oppression from us.

I was forced to divide up and partition my people because it would
have been impossible to advance with the sick people in the swampy
land, whose existence was pointed out to me and which I later found
to be exactly like that. Thus I was in no small hurry to reach the
Christians, as I had received the same news about them from several different villages. I gave an iron hoe to the cacique or leader of
Curahamara in veneration and sent him back to his pueblo or village
that was located a mile and a half from the river, as mentioned before,
along with the sick men, of whom there were twenty-seven, together
with fifty healthy ones and along with five horses. [L2v] I ordered
him to take all his people and take up peaceful residence again, as
before, and to provide good shelter to my people, who should remain
there until I returned or called them away.

I left with thirty-five men on foot and eight on horseback, along
with two hundred Indio carriers, and we traveled through many
pueblos or villages of the nations of the Caquetíos and the Guaiqueríes, of which there are many large ones populated or inhabited
by very many people. I found them to be well-defended throughout
while showing little friendship to us. Also, they did not offer anything, nor did they supply food for free. I had to endure that and
dissimulate with them. I did not stay long in any place so they would
not have time to band together. I was concerned about that more than
a little because they showed little fear of us and brashly turned out in
many places.

When I came within a half-day's journey of the pueblo or village
of Itabana, I sent ahead two Indios I had taken along from the pueblo

or village of Curahamara in order to inform the cacique or leader of my arrival and of my intentions. He had already known everything because he is a cacique or leader over many of the pueblos through which we had traveled. A lot of land as well as a lot of people of his nation of the Caquetíos are under his rule. When I arrived in his pueblo or village, which is located at a river that is not small, perhaps like the Danube,[145] and that is called Coaheri, he sat under a large canopy in his majesty, with a large number [L3r] of his subjects, all inhabitants of that village. He was not frightened of us at all. As I got off the horse, I instructed them to bring food to my men whereupon they brought us plenty of fish and bread.[146] I told the cacique or leader how I had come here to look for my associates, who had been here just a few days before, as far as I knew. However, he did not want to confirm or acknowledge that Christians, or people who just looked like us, had ever arrived there but conceded that they carried on in a village of the nation of the Guaiqueríes about a two-day journey away, located at the shore of an ocean or a lake.

I conversed and talked with him about the situation of the land and, in particular, of the lagoon or sea that we believed we might be able to see from the pueblo or village of Itabana, based on what we had been told. Just then we heard a rooster crow and several hens, which we had not seen since the day we left Coro, as the Indios do not have them.[147] And when I asked them where the chickens came from, they responded that they came from Hamadoa,[148] as the inhabitants there had negotiated and bought them there from our colleagues. Now we were certain that we would be able to reach the Christians, and we also did not doubt that the Christians had come to this pueblo or village of Itabana, which had been indicated to us by the Indios we had encountered before, as already mentioned. The Indios were not able or willing to admit that they had slain a number of the Christians, as we believed. Perhaps they were concerned that they would be punished by us for it.

145. The Danube in Federmann's native Ulm is 70 m wide; this perhaps was his point of reference.

146. Likely corn tortillas.

147. Given the remote location, the presence of a rooster and several hens is a mystery.

148. Unclear geographic reference.

Then I asked him to offer to sell me one of his female servants or slaves,[149] which is how their people who are sold are called. [L3v] I offered to give him twice the payment for the reason that I wanted to find out from her whether the Christians had been in this pueblo or village and how they had lived with them. I had no other means to find out at the time. However, they refused to give her to me even though they commonly buy and sell women to each other.

I was eager to travel to the ocean or lake, which according to their information was four miles from here. They also informed me that they did not use paths or roads to get there because the land was very swampy and covered with water and that they traveled there only in canoes; this is what they call their boats. As we had doubts, I asked myself whether it was the ocean or the body of water that Sebastian Cabot had discovered and traveled on, as discussed before. They claimed that they had not traveled by boat beyond Hamadoa, which is perhaps why they could not or did not want to tell us what we needed. They added that the water was sweet and not salty up to that point and that they could see only water and no mountains or land toward the south or sunrise,[150] as far as they could see.[151]

Since there was no option to travel there on land, as indicated before, it was impossible for me to get to the ocean or lagoon, that is, a large body of water, in this way. As we would have been deprived of the use of the horses, I could not undertake this with just a few people, not even with all the people I had brought from Coro, even if they were all healthy. Furthermore, the inhabitants revealed to us that we had little good to expect from them. They had too much practice waging war on water, [L4r] and in particular we would have been forced to use their boats without experience in navigating and steering them. This would have given them the same advantage over us on water that we would have had against them on land.

As I could not accomplish anything in this pueblo or village of Itabana and could not investigate the truth about why I had traveled there, namely to find out more about the Christians, I only stayed there until noon. I set across the river because there was a

149. "aine seiner Nauoria / oder Eschlauos." *Naboría*, a Caribbean word probably of Taíno origin, denoted a servant of an Indigenous noble. Among Spanish conquistadors, the term was used to denote personal slaves or servants.
150. This is an odd pairing since sunrise designates east.
151. Probably a large area flooded by the Río Cojedes.

mountain range on the other side,[152] perhaps a mile away. They said that the mentioned ocean or lagoon was abutting its base and could be observed from the top of the same mountain. I spent the night in a pueblo or village belonging to the nation of the Guaiqueríes. Early the next morning, I rode with two others to said mountain that was located about a mile away. Two Indios from the Guaiqueríes who also knew the language of the Caquetíos accompanied us, as the two nations live with each other, like I said before. When we reached the foot of the mountain, we found a branch of the Coaheri River that flows through the village of Itabana and meets the ocean or lagoon at this place. On the other side, we found a fishery of just a few houses belonging to the Guaiqueríes. There were a large number of Indios who came from several different villages in order to buy fish so that we doubted whether we should dare riding up to them. In order not to encourage them to rise against us, we got the three horses to swim across the river so that the water went over the saddles, and we arrived on the other side like drenched mice. [L4v] We did not want to take the risk to let the horses swim on their own and let the Indios carry us across.

When we reached the top of the mountain, we saw that the land downriver from Itabana was entirely covered with water, as the Indios had said, so we had to believe what they had told us, namely that they did not get there on land at all. However, we were unable to discern whether this body of water was a big lake or lagoon[153] or whether this was a quite well-inhabited and level land because it was covered by fog, which is common in watery and swampy places, and in particular early in the morning, as it was at the time.

After I had reviewed what was to be seen there and had returned to my people, the cacique or leader of Itabana arrived about a quarter hour later with a large number of his people, who were fully armed and painted, as they do when they go to war. We were shocked and immediately had all the horses saddled and armored in order to be prepared for defense, in case they were to take action. We could sense that he had received a report from the Guaiqueríes of this pueblo or village that I and two others had ridden to the said mountain and that he therefore believed that they could attack my people in my

152. Likely the Galeras del Baúl, a small mountain range east of El Baúl.
153. Federmann likely experienced seasonal flooding in the Venezuelan Llanos.

absence. I had him asked why he had come there. He responded that
he had a wife in a village about a quarter mile upriver whom he had
come to visit. For the rest of the day, we maintained good watch that
we set up against those inhabitants, who later proved us right. We
subsequently noticed that a large number of Indios assembled in the
pueblo or village where this [M1r] cacique or leader had gone. They
all wore clothing in the manner they customarily wear to go to war,
as you will hear later when I discuss the customs of this nation.

The Guaiqueríes, the inhabitants of this village where we had set
up camp, also left their pueblo or village, along with their women and
children; they moved and carried away everything they had in there
and assembled with said cacique, which was not a good sign. We had
to let it happen, as we did not have power over them to prevent it.
We were quite dismayed that we were facing such a large number of
enemies, as mentioned above. Furthermore, we did not see a path that
was to our advantage at the location where we were.

Therefore, around midnight, we quietly moved those Christians
who could not swim across the river with a little boat of the Indios
and got the horses to swim across. In this way, we managed to tra-
verse the river with our entire supply train and all our belongings.
We stayed there until daybreak and traveled back early in the morning toward the pueblo or village of Curahamara, where I had left the
other part of my people. When the cacique or leader and his people
wanted to assault and vanquish us in the morning at the place and
village where they had left us, they could not find us and instead saw
us move away along the riverbank across the water. They ran ahead
to a passage or pathway in a location along the bank of the river
where we had to move through. There, about fifteen hundred Indios
swam across the river to the side where we [M1v] were traveling and
lay in wait in a hidden location.

As we were moving along, only paying attention to those we could
see on the other side but not worrying about those on our side who
had come across the river, they began to attack us, front and back.
Furthermore, the cacique or leader and his seven thousand Indios,
as we estimated, were also shooting at us from the other side of the
river and attacked us with loud shouts. We battled with each other
for a long time and stabbed to death many of those who attacked us
on our side while we pushed the others back into the water. Furthermore, my crossbowmen did substantial harm to those who had

gotten into the water and to those who were with the cacique or lord on the other side of the river. After a long time, they stopped shooting and fled inland, away from the banks of the river. For that reason, we believed that maybe the cacique or leader may have been hit by one of our shooters. This is their style: as soon as their lord or commander is injured, the game is over, and their huddle gets dispersed. Only four of the Christians remained uninjured. I was shot through my shoulder as well, and two horses were hurt badly. One of them was shot with a poisoned arrow and died raging on the sixth day.

As the Indios were withdrawing from us, as mentioned before, we moved to an elevation half a mile away from the river. There we settled down in order to dress our wounds. On the same evening, we moved [M2r] to a pueblo or village we had traveled through as we moved into the area. However, we did not find anybody there. Perhaps they were concerned that we would avenge on them the violation and attack we had endured and suffered at the hands of the people from Itabana since they were subject to the same cacique or leader and of course had also participated in this battle. There, we spent the night. After we got up in the morning we set the village on fire. We did the same thing in all pueblos or villages through which we traveled and that belonged to this cacique or leader. Thus we moved along with a good deal of effort and labor with our wounded men and horses, looking more like gypsies than warriors.

On the one-and-a-half-day trip away from the Coaheri River that was mentioned before, where the nation of the Guaiqueríes begins, we reached several pueblos and villages who are not subject to the cacique or leader of Itabana. We found their inhabitants at arms and not with less pride than when we had left them. For this reason, we did not spend the night in any of their pueblos or villages. We took our necessary provisions from them during the day and settled down in the most concealed area in the field. We did this so that they could not see our injured men and our bandaged horses and notice that they had been wounded, but also so that the Indios in our supply train did not have the opportunity to pass on that information.

Early in the morning on the fifth day of February in the noted year 1531, we arrived in a pueblo or village called Carahao,[154] where the inhabitants [M2v] were not aware of our arrival. We encountered

154. Village and location are unknown.

them fully armed and very cocky. The cacique or leader of the nation of the Guaiqueríes, whose fishery was here and with whom I had closed the first friendship in this nation, was among them, along with many of his people. This was not to our liking, but we were unsure who their arms were aimed at. We did not pull back at all but rather moved straight ahead. Said cacique or leader of the Guaiqueríes accompanied me, in addition to one of the captains from the pueblo called Carahao.

In the meantime, the Christians I had left behind in Curahamara, at the time when I was traveling toward Itabana, had crossed the river as well and had set up camp near the fishery so that they would have fewer food shortages. For this cacique or leader of the pueblo or village of Curahamara had not kept his pledge but had instead departed his pueblo or village and left it deserted, contrary to what he had promised me. Therefore, the Christians did not have anybody who was trading with the Guaiqueríes and who bought the needed provisions from them. Therefore, they were forced to move their encampment to said location.

When they saw us approach from a distance, they were very happy about our arrival, as they had been shown a lot of swagger by the Guaiqueríes and therefore were worried about being raided by them. Allegedly, the Guaiqueríes also rejected orders to supply provisions or food for payment or trade and did not leave their defensive positions. As they sent out a man on horseback to tell me this, I had the cacique or leader of the [M3r] same nation and the lord of this fishery held, captured, and bound, along with the captain, as both were escorting me. I had them led into the shrubs and interrogated under torture to find out their intention behind appearing in full armor, also why they treated my people so maliciously, and why they denied them food for payment.

Rather than revealing and confessing anything, the cacique or leader endured torture under a lot of pain. Therefore, I had him shot dead[155] in plain view of the other captive, as a horrible example for him. I promised the second captive to spare his life if he told me the truth about what they had planned, conspired, and decided against my people. He confessed to me how his cacique or leader

155. The German "erschiessen" implies the use of a projectile. Federmann may have used an arquebus for theatrical effect.

from the pueblo or village of Carahao, which is part of the nation of the Caquetíos, together with the cacique or leader of the nation of the Guaiqueríes, who just had been shot dead, had decided to jointly attack and defeat the Christians that very morning, each with his own subjects. They were already preparing and setting things in motion, but our unexpected arrival hindered them. Therefore, I had an iron chain forged to hold him, along with others. I sent someone to my men who were waiting for us in their encampment by the river. They had to keep their horses and people armed because I was concerned that the Indios from the pueblo or village of Carahao, whom we had found fully armed, as mentioned before, would follow us and attack us while we were crossing the river.

[M3v] When I reached the fishery and the encampment of the Christians, we encountered about eight hundred Indios of the Guaiqueríes who were well armed and ready for war. They were waiting for their cacique or leader, whom I had shot dead, as mentioned before, and for the Caquetíos from the village of Carahao in order to attack our people. Then I ordered them to put down their weapons and to become friends again to the extent they had vowed to and agreed to the first time I was moving through the area, and furthermore, I ordered them to demonstrate this with friendly and peaceful deeds, but they proudly refused to do that. Therefore, we surrounded them with our horses and distracted them with our talk and made sure that they could not flee through the water.

Then we attacked them because we were in a beautiful plain that was to our advantage; we could not have wished for any better. We stabbed about five hundred of them, as they were very much taken by surprise because we were still discussing and negotiating a peaceful resolution with them. Therefore, they did not pay attention to what we did and were not prepared to defend themselves. We stabbed many of them on the ground until we got them to flee. The men on horseback ran into their hordes alone and pushed to the ground as many as they could. Those on foot stabbed them like pigs. Fleeing was their only option, yet they were at a disadvantage because of the speed of our horses. In the end, they were hiding in the grass, where the living were able to save themselves by hiding among those who had been stabbed. We searched for those as well, as we had done with the others, and strangled many of them. Like that, about five hundred of them perished, as mentioned above. Only those fleeing across the water [M4r] could not be fought.

Only five Christians of mine were injured, but none of them lethally, and about thirteen Indios from our supply train. Our desperate situation required this attack, and they suffered for their delinquency. For we had to worry that the Caquetíos would follow us, as we were told and informed by the tortured Indios. Since they had decided and resolved to do this, it was better and to our advantage to fight with a few men of theirs rather than a lot of them. Now that we had overcome them, which we could do using our advantage, the others would be less powerful to withstand us. It was a good thing for us that their assault backfired on them.

We remained there all day long and into the night. We could not risk crossing the river during the day because we were concerned about being attacked by the Caquetíos and about being separated, as some of ours already had crossed the river. As night fell, and we no longer had to be concerned about an attack, we made the horses swim across the river, followed by the men who could not swim on rafts that we had made out of shields, pulling them with ropes from one bank of the river to the other. Early the next morning, I arrived in the pueblo or village of Curahamara. I did not encounter anybody and instead found the village deserted. This was the reason, as I reported before, why the Christians, namely my people that I had left there, were forced to move their encampment to the river.

I had this cacique or leader [M4v] pursued, but I was unable to catch up with him. For that reason, I moved on four miles from there to a different village that I also found deserted and depopulated, just as I had found and left it when I first had come through here. Therefore, I remained there until the third day, and in the meantime, I sent several Christians on horseback and on foot back to the pueblo or village of Curahamara in order to assault it at night.

So it happened. In the village, they found the cacique or leader with all his people. He had returned to live there again, believing that we had moved along and hoping that he therefore was safe from us. What he did is exactly what we had planned, namely enticing him to return after we had traveled away from his pueblo or village. Thus my men captured the cacique or leader and twenty-three other persons, men and women, most of them leaders or nobles. As

punishment for having broken his pledge to me three times, I had
him put in chains and led him, as well as the others I had captured
with him, all the way to Coro like this. I distributed the women
among the Christians to be of service to them.

In this village, I was hit by a fever so that I was unable to move
along quickly. Therefore, I moved slowly from one village to the next,
all of which we found desolate and depopulated, up to the pueblo of
Cathary,[156] where we had been before. There, the inhabitants received
us very well and renewed the same friendship they had provided
to us before. We stayed with them for two days and remembered
the other path [N1r] through which we could reach the lagoon or
sea through the nation of the Coyones. They instructed us that we
could reach it unimpeded if we always stayed close to the mountains
because it was not swampy there. They also reported to us about a
great river called Temeri,[157] which they said was two bow shots wide
and very deep but possible to cross with rafts or by other means.

On the tenth of February, I came back to the pueblo or village of
Acarigua, where I had stayed fifteen days before. I found the inhabitants quietly in their houses, just as I had left them. They showed
more joy than displeasure about our arrival. Therefore, I donated to
the cacique or leader two beautiful India women I had captured in the
pueblo or village of Curahamara. I stayed in this village until the sixteenth day, as I was hoping to get rid of my fever, which caused me to
experience both heat and cold,[158] so that I could continue my journey
to the lagoon or sea by way of the abovementioned Temeri River.

Halfway through my sixteen-day stay in Acarigua, I sent a
number of men on horseback and on foot to the mountains of the
Coyones, along with a number of Indios we had captured from them
before, in order to gain their friendship by offering to return their
captives to them. I also had them told, through their own people,
who were my prisoners, what kind of people and how many we had
dismembered and slain in Itabana on the same journey because they
resisted us and [N1v] despised our friendship but also, on the other
hand, how we remained faithful and gave good treatment to those

156. Federmann has not mentioned this unknown town by name before.
157. Likely the Río Portuguesa, which had different names among Indigenous
people, such as Guanaguanare and El Temeri.
158. Recurring high fever and chills both are symptoms of malaria.

who surrendered to us. Yet, all of this did not want to take root with them, nor did it make them forget past harm. None of the many ways we tried to turn them into friends had an effect.

They left their villages and spent the night in the most rugged mountains, where they could not be approached on carts, let alone on horses. Therefore, we had to forgo their friendship, as much as we would have liked to be in agreement with them because we had intended at the time to travel through their land to the aforementioned lagoon or sea. My illness and that of many of my men continued and persisted, yet there was no improvement in sight because of the unusual diet and the absence of all remedies that would help a sick person get well again. I therefore decided to return to the coast or shore of the ocean,[159] but not by traveling over the mountains the same way we had come here. From there, we could send a message to Coro and also request and demand what we needed, along with a reinforcement of fresh people.

We left Acarigua on the twenty-seventh of February and traveled through the nation of the Cuibas, where we had traveled on the outward journey. We encountered a number of pueblos or villages, some of them inhabited and others deserted. Those who retreated were concerned that we were only loyal to them when we first moved through in order to deceive us, but now that we were returning, we would capture them and take them along with us as slaves or [N2r] as sold people. However, it was not opportune nor necessary for us to lose much time by mollifying the fugitives about their fear or by pursuing them. For those who did not trust us and therefore left their pueblos or villages had enough examples of how we dealt with those who awaited us in their pueblos or villages.

Here I have to report a deception that happened to us in one of their pueblos or villages. Namely, we arrived in a pueblo or village of the nation of the Cuibas, where we had not been before, because we did not want to take the way back through Barquisimeto, where we had been before. However, we did not find any Indios in this village and therefore were searching for them. Two India women were captured on the street in a place where they did not notice us. I sent one of them to their cacique or leader with a number of gifts to get him to come to me and engage in friendship. As you already heard, I

159. The Atlantic Ocean.

frequently had done the same with others before. The India woman returned and brought me a small, precious piece of gold. It was a demonic image of the kind they wear as ornaments on their chests. She also told me that her cacique or leader was ill and could not appear in person and was asking me to accept the gift and to return the two women to him. I responded that he should have himself carried to me in his own pueblo or village, even though he was sick, and to bring along his people, [N2v] and to resume living there peacefully. He would have to do all of this anyway after I was gone. Then I would return the captive women to him.

The next morning, an Indio arrived with about forty people. He had himself carried in a hammock as if he was the lord or cacique of the village, and we certainly thought that he was the cacique or leader. I tried to have him talked into occupying his village again and returned the two women to him. Unknown to us, he took off with all his people during the following night and left the hammock in which he had been carried hanging in the house, so that we did not find a single human being in the morning. From that we deduced that he was not the cacique or leader. Instead he must have been an ordinary Indio or a slave and sold servant and that he was sent to us by the cacique or leader to take the risk in case we did not remain true to our word and to get a release for the two women. This was set up to secure the women's release since one them must have been the wife or a relative of the cacique, for if they had they been ordinary women, they would have been left to us.

Thus we were deceived by this Indio in a fashion we had not yet encountered on our journey. Here their evil and false lust to betray can be detected.

As much as we would have liked to punish them for this, we nevertheless did not want to lose more time by pursuing them. As we did not have a travel guide for the day [N3r] ahead of us, we moved toward the province of Barquisimeto. In these pueblos or villages, we encountered the inhabitants the way we had left them. There we settled for our night's rest and rested all evening.

[Chapter 12] The Nation of the Caquetíos. Of this populous, beautiful province of the Caquetíos. Of the size of their villages, number of inhabitants, men usable for war, their well-proportioned bodies, and the beauty of their women. How the Christians moved through it, encountering

little friendship and goodwill with them, and also were feared very little. Furthermore, how they had to prevail in fights and battles at the end, a cacique stabbed (in order to prevent unrest) and many of his people slain and captured, and also how they and their belongings barely escaped with difficulty and distress.

The following day, it was the first day of March, we left and moved through a valley that is located between two mountains. On the mountains toward sunset, the Ciparicotos lived and toward the sunrise, the Hitotos. However, the flat valley, which is four miles wide and reaches from one mountain range to the other, is owned by the Caquetíos, who are not friends with those in Barquisimeto even though they are from the same nation. This is why there are no villages within one-and-a-half-day trips from Barquisimeto; instead the land is depopulated and deserted. Nevertheless, we found a number of old buildings of their kind along the way [N3v] that were destroyed and burned, where pueblos and villages had been in former times. The people in Barquisimeto did not want to give me guides for the mentioned reason that they have enemies on all sides and were concerned that they would have to move out in full force in order to have them returned. We were not interested in that at all, as we had interpreters ourselves in the language of the Caquetíos. Also it was hard to miss the way as long as one stayed in the flat part of the valley.

We settled down next to a river for the first night. In the morning, we were quietly exploring the paths forward when we encountered about 150 Indios, men and women, who were working in their fields without taking note of us. We captured them, and when we approached their village with them, the Indios from this village or pueblo approached us in full armor. They had been alerted and notified by an Indio who had seen my men on horseback from afar. About seven thousand of them, as we estimated, assembled outside of a pueblo or village, as they believed that we had come to raid them. While the ones in the fields were watching, they confronted us brazenly and also stood in formation, ready to shoot at us.

I had them informed why I seized the people on the field, in addition to whatever was helpful to keep peace. I also returned their prisoners to them. We had a long talk with them, but they remained impudent and did not want to be diverted from their plan to wage war on us [N4r] and to shoot at us. Both sides would have had little gain from this because, on one hand, we were on a plain where horses were very helpful to us, but on the other hand, their people were spread out and not in one place so that they could have surrounded us better than we could have surrounded them. When they finally could be convinced to cede their favorable position to us and to return to their village, we followed them and set up camp with them in their village. I sent tokens of appreciation to the cacique or leader and thereby assuaged his audacity. The same evening we moved a mile away to a different village whose inhabitants did not resist us because I had them informed beforehand about my arrival and reasons for being there. I also took along with me the cacique from the last pueblo or village.

So far on our journey, we had not learned about the size and the large number of inhabitants of these pueblos or villages nor what a cocky, proud, and belligerent people they are. In a single day, they can assemble twenty thousand Indios who can wage war, as we estimated. Even though all these pueblos or villages are of the same nation, they are not under the rule of a single lord. As they are near and very close to each other, as said before, I concluded that there was a very large number of inhabitants in close proximity and that they would be able to resist a mighty troop of Christians or, at least, to instill fear. Yet there is a different sense in the present pueblo [N4v] of this valley, even though there are as many inhabitants here, because they do not agree or conform with each other. Rather, just two, three, or four pueblos each are confederated or allied with one another, which is why they are less powerful than those in Barquisimeto. However, there is no doubt that they would band together, confederate, and ally if war were to be waged against them and if they would not be able to fight back adequately.

They have large villages, often half a mile long, but these only have one lane or two, at the most. Usually five, six, or up to eight residents,[160] with wives and children, live in one house. They are a people of very good height and proportion, also of strong disposition and physical perfection. Furthermore, they have very beautiful women with good posture, which is why we call this valley and province that the Indios call Vararida, *El valle de las damas*, which in German is

---

160. Federmann's term "haußvolck" is the German *Hausvolk*, a legal term including all members of a household, including servants.

Valley of the Ladies. In this nation or province, the use of poisonous herbs and plants ends, and they indeed only use projectiles alone, not with any of the poisons, like those in Coro.

Then we traveled through three of their villages that are in this confederation or alliance, although there are more of them that were not on our way. They exhibited very bad friendship to us, as they relied on their large numbers or masses. In addition, they never gave us a present, even though they have a lot of wealth. In many of the pueblos or villages, they even demanded substantial payments from us to cover our basic food needs, which we nonetheless did not give to them.

On the third day of March,[161] [O1r] we reached another pueblo or village, which was an enemy of the pueblos or villages we had just traveled through. Only with great effort and labor did we manage to keep them peaceful. We had a little skirmish with them in the first village that we raided, yet we eventually got them on the right track. We came to rest there and wanted to stay a day because I had a violent fever and could barely keep myself on the horse. However, they wanted to send us away and lead us to other villages belonging to their friends. They would have preferred to see the hail fall on their neighbor's house since we surely were more than thunder and lightning for them. We let them, as the first friends of this alliance, persuade us as not to provoke their ill will but also because their pueblo or village was not situated in a location where we could see far around us or could set up our guard as our needs required.

I need to stop for brevity's sake, although I made little use of brevity in this report. Yet I will strive to write only as much as will not be irritating to the reader.

We also traveled through the pueblos or villages of the other confederation or alliance, and now we were beginning to encounter other villages, the last ones of the nation of the Caquetíos. We were forced to make friends with them, like with the previous villages. We unwittingly encountered a pueblo or village around seven o'clock in the morning, a time when they usually eat breakfast. They were startled, as they did not know anything about us [O1v] until we overwhelmed them while they were gorging. All of them ran into their houses and

---

161. The texts says the third day of February, but this is in error, as the previous date mentioned is February twenty-seventh.

locked themselves up. I managed to convince them that they did not have to worry about us, and they came out of their houses. They also opened their houses out of fear, as I threatened to set fire to their village. I therefore thought that they were pacified. I occupied a number of houses with my people in locations that served to our advantage. We settled in, thinking that we would stay for a day, cooperate with the cacique or leader, and then move peacefully through these pueblos or villages who were in the alliance and confederation of this cacique or leader.

In spite of that, the Christians who patrolled the lanes and kept watch told me how women and children of this village were, quietly and one after the other, absconding from the pueblo or village. This did not signal peace to us, as the Indios only do this when they are at war and when they plan dreadful things. Therefore, I had the cacique or leader come to me, and I reprimanded him for the removal of the women and children. I also had the Indios brought to me whom I had captured on this journey in the village of Curahamara and in other places and had brought along with me, forged in chains. I let the cacique or leader be informed that we had captured these Indios for reasons exactly like this, and that this would also happen to him if he did not change his behavior. He believed that he would be apprehended, captured, and placed in chains right away, [O2r] which was not my intent. I had only raised that point so that he would stop the removal of the women and children.

He immediately shot up from the chair on which he sat across from me and ran away quickly. I managed to seize him so that there would not be an uprising in the pueblo or village. When he was grabbed by the Christians and believed to be a captive, he started to scream loudly, calling his people to help him. To prevent worse, one of the Christians drove a sword through him on my order. We engaged in a vicious battle with the inhabitants of this pueblo or village and slew and captured many of them, until we managed to get them to flee from their pueblo or village.

In the meantime, while we were battling the others and did not pay attention, a number of his men were hiding in the buhío (this is how their houses are called) where I had taken up residence, where I had given commands to the cacique or leader, and where I had threatened to put him in chains, as indicated before. They were tucked away in a high storage loft that stood in the middle of the house and was

supported by four posts the height of three men; they use it to store
their grain or maize. After we were done battling them, we wanted
to remove our belongings and the crates containing all the gold we
had captured on this journey from this buhío. We wanted to move
away quickly before the pueblos or villages of this confederation and
alliance could mobilize and attack us, for my people were very tired,
and many of them were ill and also wounded after the battle that just
had been fought. At that moment, the Indios who [O2v] were hiding
in this *barbacoa*,[162] that is how it is called, moved. They believed that
we were looking for them so we could treat them like the others but
that we were not able to find them. However, that was not our intention, as we knew nothing of their presence, and had they not given
themselves away, we would not have noticed them.

As we entered the buhío or house obliviously, they shot at us as if
shooting at targets and shot and injured five of us, including shooting
me through the shoulder several times. They forced us to back off to
a safe spot because they had control over us from above. Thereupon
I sent in five men who had to cut down the barbacoa and protect
themselves underneath it because it was standing freely on just four
posts so that a man, no matter how tall, could stand upright underneath it. We could not burn down the buhío or house along with the
Indios since we had to safeguard our goods that we still had in there.
The Christians did a lot of shouting in the buhío or house but did not
achieve anything, one of them just impeding the other. I got a little
impatient because they took too long and deprived us of our advantage over the Indios before they could attack us.

Therefore, I ran into the buhío or house underneath the barbacoa.
After one stake was cut down, the barbacoa began to lean, and the
weight of the grains that slid to the sagging side pushed the barbacoa
over entirely, and the Indios fell down as a result. I protected myself
with my buckler or shield, and I was just about to drive the sword
through the body of an Indio. He gave me such a powerful blow with
a [O3r] *macana*,[163] which is how their wooden swords are called, that
he cracked off and shattered a piece of my buckler, which was made of

162. The term "barbacoa" designates an elevated platform supported by reeds or
sticks and used as a granary.
163. "Macana" is a Taíno word referring to various wooden weapons used in Central and South America, like clubs or cudgels.

the bottom of a barrel, about two fingers wide.[164] When I stabbed him again, not having noticed in the commotion that a piece was missing from my buckler, I did not protect myself sufficiently, and he hit me with a strike on my head so that I fell to the ground in front of him. He would have taken my life if others had not jumped in to assist me and executed the Indio. I was lying there unconscious for two hours. We stayed there overnight with good guards because we were worried that we would be assaulted in this village. These Indios in the barbacoa, while only twelve in number, did more harm to us and wounded more of my people than all the others.

[Chapter 13] The Nation of the Ciparicotos. How the Christians intended to travel through this nation and were led astray by the captive guides and leaders into a wilderness and thicket with the intention of making them die of hunger so that they would avenge and vindicate their captivity and the death of their slain people. Also how the Christians, when they discovered the deception, had three[165] of them chopped up to induce fear and terror in the others, whereupon the others steadfastly stayed with their plan and rather wanted to die with their own than being prisoners. And what hunger the Christians faced so that they all nearly perished because of starvation, whereupon they ate a captured jaguar for the sustenance of their lives, until they reached a village after erring around for a long time, were strengthened with provisions, and also saved their lives so they could move along.

[O3v] We departed early in the morning, an hour before daybreak, not to travel through the land of the Caquetíos but rather along the mountains, through that of their enemies, the Ciparicotos. I had one of the Indios tied alive to the column of the barbacoa in the buhío or house where the eleven dead Indios lay. He had to tell the Caquetíos who returned there that I had punished the cacique or leader and also the inhabitants of this pueblo or village because they did not want to be loyal to me and because they dared move out of the village. Furthermore, those who did the same to me could also expect the same, but those who were loyal to me would receive good treatment or support and good friendship from me, as he could observe himself.

---

164. "Zwerchfinger," *Querfinger*, is a unit of measurement that corresponds to the width of a finger—that is, about 2 cm.

165. The text later mentions that only two Indios were killed [O4r].

We used a number of Indios we had captured in this village and took them with us in chains as guides. They led us through a thicket until we lost the trail. Yet they marched along as they persuaded us that we would reach the Ciparicotos on a different path. Then the Indios reported to us that this trail was overgrown because they used it rarely and only if they wanted to raid each other as enemies but not otherwise. This was not true, however, because the trail we were traveling on was used by the Caquetíos solely to bring wood for the construction of their houses. As we did not find another trail on this day, in spite of the assurances of our guides, and night fell upon us, we settled down next to a creek. We made do with the little provisions [O4r] or food that we carried with us, which we quickly used up since we had counted on reaching a pueblo or village on the same day. I also had the Indios interrogated under torture, yet they insisted unanimously on their original tale.

The next day, we still could not find a trail. We followed the sun through the forest toward sunrise, and hope left us entirely, as we saw ourselves betrayed by the Indios. We had traveled the entire day without having eaten, and we also had no water other than what we had taken from where we had camped. We were unable to pry information out of our guides, neither amicably nor under torture. Therefore, I had two of them hacked to death to instill fear in the others. Yet, this did not help at all, as they rather wanted to be stabbed to death than be our prisoners. They also had showed us this path just to lead us astray so that we would die of hunger. They wanted to take revenge on us and nearly were successful.

Full of fear, we knew how to move neither forward nor backward, as all of us were without courage because of the lack of food and our hunger and, in particular, because we had a great need for water. We also were in a thicket where we did not know a path, nor could we find the way back. Furthermore, it was difficult to move the horses because they were thirsty. When some men I had ordered to climb the tallest trees in the forest indicated seeing a meadow half a mile away lying to one side [O4v], we moved there. After traveling just a short distance, the dogs[166] we had with us signaled from fairly far away so that we believed that we had come across a wild boar, as

---

166. This is the only time Federmann mentions dogs. Other conquistadors used fighting dogs. If that was their purpose here, Federmann concealed that.

there were many of them here. Therefore, I sent out people to follow the dogs in the hope of hunting something so we could remedy and alleviate our hunger. We also hoped that we would reach water, which would have raised the expectation that we would find a pueblo or village.

When my people reached the dogs amidst a lot of roaring, they encountered a strong jaguar,[167] of which kind will be said more later, standing in front of the dogs, already having torn apart two of them. The Christians did not dare to attack it. Only a monk,[168] who was also among them, charged it in order to stab it. As the jaguar wanted to pounce on him, it got entangled in a liana,[169] of which there are many in these forests. This is a tough plant, like a willow, that grows over trails and from one tree to the next like tightened ropes. This was the monk's luck, for otherwise he would have paid dearly for his excessive bravery. The other Christians, his comrades, rushed to him and stabbed the animal. One of them drove his pike into its mouth, whereupon it bit off the iron tip of the spike in the middle as if it was lead. After they had stabbed, shot, and killed it, they loaded it on a horse and brought it to us. It is the largest jaguar I had seen in the Indies. The horse [P1r] had enough work to carry it; its color was pale yellow because of its age.

When we reached the meadow mentioned before, we could not find a path there either. But we were able to look around and believed that the land was inhabited. We moved on and found a small creek that was running through the woods at the foot of a mountain. There we set up camp because our health and welfare depended on it. If we had we not reached water that night, we would have spent a miserable night, and we would have been worried about having to leave behind many men due to thirst for many already now could only keep up with great difficulty.

Once we quenched our thirst, we felt our hunger more urgently. As we had nothing else, they ate the jaguar even though it is not usually eaten for it is a smelly and quite unhealthy meat. I believe

167. "Tigerthier."

168. This is the only time Federmann explicitly mentions the presence of clergy, although earlier references to the conversion of natives implies their presence. The presence of clergy on *entradas* was required.

169. "Weschuco," Spanish *bejuco*, English *liana*, refers to a long-stemmed woody vine that often reaches the tree canopy.

that our stomachs would have devoured wooden logs, in particular as each of us was only allotted a piece barely the size of two nuts, as we had 450[170] people in our supply train. The jaguar, however, was the size of a calf that is half a year old.

We left on the third day, as we were most interested in finding populated or inhabited land. At around two o'clock in the afternoon, we encountered a trail that led from the mountain to the plain. Even though we had traveled from the morning until two o'clock in the afternoon to reach this path, it was no more than two [P1v] miles from where we had spent the night. This is how poorly I was able to move with my people.

I sent out four men on horseback to explore this trail and followed more slowly with the rest of the people. They came back and told us that they had reached a pueblo but that they did not know to what nation it belonged. Furthermore, the inhabitants had noticed them and were restless. That did not suit us well, yet the positives outweighed the negatives. We were energized and reached the pueblo or village, but we did not find anyone, as the inhabitants had already departed. However, the entire village was full of good provisions and foods. They did not have enough time to take it when they were fleeing. This was more useful to us than the presence or companionship of the natives. We set up camp there and stayed until the fourth day, making up for our misery.

This is the greatest hunger that we experienced. Had it lasted another night and, in particular, had we not found said little creek, we would have had to be worried that only a few of us would have reached Coro and returned there, for we would have lacked the strength to reach food, particularly those on foot. While we also suffered a shortage of food supplies when we traveled from Barquisimeto to the nation of the Cuibas, as you heard before, it was a different situation.

During the days when we had our encampment there, I sent out a number of Christians to check out the trails in the mountains.[171] They captured three Indios from the nation of the Ciparicotos [P2r]

---

170. "Fünffthalb hundert," literally "four and half of the fifth hundred" (450). This is a large number, given that Federmann started out with 126 European mercenaries and 100 carriers. Later, he reported having 250 Indians [G1r].

171. Likely the Sierra de Aroa.

and brought them to me. However, we could not talk to them, nor could they understand us. Instead, we signaled through gestures and however else we could communicate that we had not come to harm them. I also made sure that they received good treatment and support. Furthermore, I sent one of them with gifts or presents home to his cacique or leader.

On the same day, a single Indio came to our encampment, who was from the nation of the Ciparicotos but also knew the language of the Caquetíos. He brought me a present of gold that his cacique or leader sent to me so that I would free the prisoners. I learned from him about the nature of this land and found out that we were only five days away from the coast or shore of the ocean. Then I sent him back to his cacique or leader in order to tell him that he should come to me and that he should calmly settle again in his pueblo or village. I had this Indio apprised by the other Indios, to make it look like this did not happen on my order or with my knowledge, about the discipline we meted out to those who were disobedient and resisted us but also about the good and friendly treatment and support we provided for those who surrendered to us.

Thus the cacique or leader came with all his people and with equipment and supplies and settled back into his village, and we confirmed peace with them. During the following three days, we peacefully traveled through this nation and many of its pueblos or villages and found good accommodations with them. On the twelfth day of March, we left the mountains [P2v] and reached the nation of the Caquetíos again, located in the plains. These Caquetíos, however, had left their villages deserted and were hiding in the mountains. As they live close to the coast or shore, many of them had been abducted, betrayed, and sold by the Christians on pirate ships from Santo Domingo and from other islands. They believed that we also had arrived on pirate ships so that we could not engage with any of them, neither in peace nor in war.

Therefore, I sent off a number of the Caquetíos I had led with me from Coro to search for the surrounding Indios and to inform them that we were the Christians who lived in Coro in the land of the cacique or leader called Manaure[172] and also that we had not come to rob

---

172. Manaure, "Manuaury," an important cacique of the coastal regions between Coro and Maracaibo, had entered an agreement with Juan Martínez de Ampiés, the first governor of Venezuela.

or harm them. We could assume that along the coast or shore of the ocean, the inhabitants would have heard news about us Christians in Coro. The Indios we had sent out soon found the inhabitants, for a mouse knows well the hiding places of other mice. They brought with them many of the Indios who exhibited joy about our arrival and gave us all kinds of presents. They also complained to me about a pirate ship that had been recently with them at the coast or shore of the ocean. They raided and took many of the nation of the Hitotos who live in the mountains four miles from there and are the enemies of these Caquetíos. This is why they were worried about our arrival and why they had deserted their villages.

[P3r] After that I traveled on a large river called Yaracuy, which is no smaller than the Rhine River, with good accompaniment and support from these Caquetíos, all the way to the shore of the ocean to a pueblo or village called Xaragua,[173] which is located at the coast or shore of the North Sea,[174] eighty miles from Coro toward sunrise.

From this pueblo or village we traveled along the coast or shore of the ocean toward Coro to a village called Martinico.[175] There, we reached the first Indios of the Caquetíos, who before had made friends with our Christians of Coro through a captain called Bartolomé Zarco[176] who had been sent out from Coro a year ago in order to make friends with the Indios who live along the coast or shore of the ocean. From this village, I sent out a Christian, along with twelve Indios, on the ocean in a canoe, which is what the boats of the Indios are called, toward Coro to the governor, who presumably had returned from Santo Domingo.

I gave him this account, news, and report of this journey and of our performance, which all was annotated by a public notary or official registrar who also traveled along on this journey[177] and who took notes on what took place from one village to the next. An order

173. Likely located where the Río Yaracuy joins the Golfo Triste—that is, the Caribbean Sea.

174. The Atlantic Ocean; here the Caribbean Sea.

175. This town is not known today.

176. Bartolomé Zarco was *alcalde ordinario*, an administrative official of the council of Coro.

177. "Nottario [oder] Scribono publico" refers to a *notario* or *escribano público* in the Spanish system. This is the first mention of a Spanish official in the text, presumably the notary Antonio de Naveros. Officials of the Spanish Crown routinely participated in such incursions.

and decree in all Indian lands by His Imperial Majesty requires the submission of a credible report to His Imperial Majesty about all and everything that occurs in the Indies. This I translated into German here, most briefly and according to the letter. Yet, [P3v] I could not avoid disclosing more about the circumstances of a number of things since this report was written in the Spanish language on location where the nature and many aspects of the manners and customs of the Indian lands are well known. If this translation[178] was written with brevity and according to the letter or if it had followed the Spanish language closely, it would be entirely incomprehensible and would have been much too obscure for those to whom such things are entirely alien.

[Chapter 14] Return from the back country to Coro.
When the governor learned that we were approaching and that many of our men were injured or ill, he demanded that we traveled back to Coro so that we had to travel sixty-five miles along the shore of the ocean. All of it was through the nation of the Caquetíos, who already had become our friends, for reasons mentioned before, and from whom we received good treatment or support and whatever goods they had to offer. I sent many of the weakest of the sick men back to Coro on the ocean in two canoes, which are the boats of the Indios, so that they would reach helpful remedies or assistance for their illnesses more expeditiously. With the other part of the people, I moved toward Coro on land. [P4r] On the way, we made friends with a nation called Aticares whose people live at the edge of the mountains and who are confederated or allied with two pueblos or villages of the Caquetíos, and we received presents from them.

On the seventeenth day of the month of March in the year 1531, my journey, praise the Lord, found a good and happy end back in Coro, where I found the governor.[179] On this journey, we traveled, as you heard, seventy miles through mountainous terrain in the nations of the Jirajaras, Ayamanes, and Achagua. There we reached the plains and moved inland through the nations of the Caquetíos, Cuibas and Guaiqueríes, all the way to the last pueblo or village called Itabana, located an estimated fifty miles straight toward the South Sea in the

---

178. "Tranßlado," based on the Spanish *traslado*.
179. Ambrosius Dalfinger.

direction of midday. On the return journey from Itabana, we moved on the same path we had arrived on, up to Barquisimeto, which I do not add to my calculations. From there, we took our path through the Caquetío land of the Vararida valley and through the Ciparicote land up to the village of Xaragua, on the shore of the North Sea, which is thirty-five miles. And from this pueblo or village, it is sixty-five miles to Coro. This is how far into the country we traveled on this journey. No Christian had ever traveled from twelve miles outside of Coro, in the nation of the Jirajaras, to where we reached the pueblo or village of Martinico on the shore of the North Sea. We alone were the first ones on this journey.

[Chapter 15] Return to Spain from Coro. [P4v]

I remained in Coro until the ninth day of December of the same year, in part to wait out my illness, as my fever had returned. I traveled to Santo Domingo in order to travel to Spain and onward to Germany at the request of the Welsers, my masters. I was fortunate to arrive in Santo Domingo with good winds on the eighteenth day of the same month. There I remained in order to wait for Sebastian Rentz until the fourth day of April of the thirty-second year, when we left Santo Domingo in the name of God and with good winds, which, however, only lasted that day. The headwind that seized us the following night forced us to sail to an island called Isla de Mona.[180] We remained there until the second day, that was the seventh day of said month. We sailed off in the evening with some good winds and some head-winds, which could not have been softer, until the ninth day of April.

Late in the evening, a large and violent storm or tempest arose, which lasted until the twelfth day of April, that is, three days. It forced us not only to take in the sails but also to perform all the repairs or else to allow the waves to knock us back and forth. [Q1r] We incessantly bailed the water that the high waves of the ocean tossed into our ship and that was augmented by the torrential rain, which made the people on the ship so tired and weak. In this distress, we also were not able nor allowed to keep a fire in the ship in order to cook and therefore had to make do with dry bread. Due to the frailty and the cold from which we all suffered greatly and terribly, we were nearly unable to perform the necessary work to save the ship or to

---

180. The island is located halfway between Hispaniola and Puerto Rico.

suffer it any longer, as we stood at the forty-third degree,[181] and the wind blew from the north, that is, from midnight, which is the coldest of all winds.

On the third day, the great force or strength of this storm or tempest subsided, and the winds got a little calmer. Thus, the labor of bailing water was not so overwhelming anymore, and also the angry sea got calmer. A fire to cook now could be maintained, and our past exertion should have been forgotten. However, the headwind that nearly prevented us from continuing our journey did not stop nor abate, although it gradually decreased from day to day. Finally, on the ninth day, that was the twenty-first day of the month of April of the year indicated, a good and happy wind that was very welcome to us started to blow, which helped and aided us to continue our journey, as it was pleasing to God.

[Q1v] Here, I cannot neglect to report an event that happened on the twenty-fifth day of said April, a day with very beautiful sunshine and also a calm and quiet ocean. Two crossbow shots in front of the ship, we saw a whirl of ocean water rise as high as a fairly tall building.[182] This is counter to the nature of the ocean, and no mariner nor sailor has ever seen or heard about anything like this before. When the pilot, which is what the commander of the ship is called, saw this, he instinctively assumed it to be a mountain in the ocean against which the water was beating. With all people shouting loudly and greatly scared, he quickly ordered to take in the sails, for had it been a mountain, which the pilot or leader thought it to be, the danger of death would have been closer than the conservation of our lives. As the mariners or sailors already were at work and in the process of taking in the sails for our welfare and recovery or rescue, the twister, while intensifying and growing bigger, moved over to one side in front of our ship. This filled us with considerable joy, as we had experienced agony and horror at its first sight. For had this been a mountain, as said before, or simply what it turned out to be but approaching us, reaching the ship, and hitting it, it would have pushed down the ship without redress, and our well-being would have been curtailed and cut down.

---

181. 43rd meridian west.
182. A waterspout.

I wanted to report this here because it is one of the most significant and wondrous things [Q2r] that I encountered on this entire Indian journey. The mariners or sailors in our ship, also the Portuguese we encountered in the Azores, as well as those we told in Seville, all marveled about this as something never seen nor heard of before. It resembled ignited and well-burning water because of its nature, swelling, and rapid course, even though it was just water and in the water.

We sailed on, and on the twenty-first day of May of the above-mentioned year, we reached the Azores, located 350 miles from Seville in Spain. They belong to the king of Portugal, and there are seven islands, one of them called Terceira. We approached and sailed into the port and restocked our provisions. We had a deficiency and shortage of water and provisions and food, as we had sailed for an unusually long time, in part because of headwinds and storms or tempests and in part because of a lull and lack of wind and of the very still weather that could not move us along.

However, we found great hunger on this island so that many inhabitants of the island had to move to Portugal, as they were suffering from hunger. The reason of this famine was that in the winter before last, grains were shipped to Portugal, as there were hungry years there, and this island was stripped too much. However, we were able to secure as much as we wanted through good friends the captain [Q2v] of our ship had on this island but for ample payment. We presumed that this would allow us to get to Spain and to the desired port as long as provisions and food would be rationed in a judicious way. As indicated before, we still had to travel 350 miles, which we could sail in twelve days in good winds.

While we left with good winds, fortune was against us. Because of the lack of any wind, we sat in our ship in the ocean for nine days in complete calm and entirely without wind. Only on the ninth day of June, this was on the sixteenth day after we had sailed from the island of Terceira, we identified the first land of Portugal, called Cape St. Vincent. Then we traveled along the coast or shore of the Algarve to continue or complete our journey. However, the wind prevented us from doing that, and we had to stop at a Portuguese port called Faro. Because of the lack and depletion of provisions and food, we could no longer endure a delay or postponement in feeding the ship.

When we jumped ashore at this port or harbor, we were informed by the inhabitants of that village that six pirate ships of the Moors, referred to as *fustas* and *galiots*,[183] were striking around at this coast or shore in order to ambush and rob the ships that were traveling through. Apparently the day before, they challenged a small local ship that was loaded with iron [Q3r] and chased it back into port. We had to carefully appraise the danger emanating from these pirate ships that we had to overcome, if we were targeted by them, particularly considering that our ship was heavily loaded and therefore not as well prepared to defend itself as the ships of the Moors, which were only loaded with gunpowder, artillery, and whatever serves to destroy other ships, and therefore the Moors ran their ships with only a small load. We hardly could offer them opposition or resistance with a fully loaded ship, particularly since they took along warriors for that purpose, which were greatly lacking on our ship.

Therefore, we resolved to put on land all gold and pearls that were on this ship, belonging to different people and also to His Imperial Majesty, which all was worth about 70,000 ducats. Nine of us, including Sebastian Rentz of Ulm and I, traveled on a small boat on a river from this village of Faro all the way to the small city of Ayamonte, seven miles away. There, we took horses and rode to Seville on land, twenty-five miles from Ayamonte. We sent the ship on the ocean straight to Cádiz and on to Seville, where it arrived well and without being attacked by the Moors.

[Chapter 16] Return to Augsburg from Spain. [Q3v]

This is the end of my journey from Seville to the Indies and back from there to Seville, where we arrived well on the sixteenth day of June in the year 1532. From there, both Sebastian Rentz and I traveled to the court of the Spanish empress, which at the time was based in Medina del Campo, a city that is located in Castile. It is twenty-three miles from Seville.[184] From there, we traveled toward and through Asturias, then Gascony and France, through Toulouse and

---

183. "Fuscy vnd Galliotas." Both *fusta* and *galiot* are narrow, light, and fast ships powered by both oars and sail.

184. This must be in error. The direct distance from Seville to Medina del Campo is 446 km.

Lyon. From Medina to there is about 213 miles, and 90 miles from Lyon to Augsburg. There we arrived happily and well on the last day of August of said year, God the Lord be praised.

End of this Indian History.

Printed in Haguenau by Sigmund Bund etc.

SELECTED BIBLIOGRAPHY

Adorno, Rolena, and Patrick Charles Pautz. *Alvar Núñez Cabeza de Vaca: His Account, His Life, and the Expedition of Pánfilo de Narváez.* 3 vols. Lincoln: University of Nebraska Press, 1999.

Arvelo, Lilliam. "Change and Persistence in Aboriginal Settlement Patterns in the Quíbor Valley, Northwestern Venezuela (Sixteenth to Nineteenth Centuries)." *Ethnohistory* 47, nos. 3–4 (2000): 669–704.

Asúa, Miguel de, and Roger Kenneth French. *A New World of Animals: Early Modern Europeans on the Creatures of Iberian America.* Aldershot: Ashgate, 2005.

Brendecke, Arndt. "Der 'oberste Kosmograph und Chronist Amerikas': Über einen Versuch der Monopolisierung von historischer Information." In *Zwischen Wissen und Politik: Archäologie und Genealogie frühneuzeitlicher Vergangenheitskonstruktionen,* edited by Frank Bezner and Kirsten Mahlke, 353–73. Heidelberg: Universitätsverlag Winter, 2011.

Denzer, Jörg. *Die Konquista der Augsburger Welser-Gesellschaft in Südamerika (1528–1556): Historische Rekonstruktion, Historiografie und lokale Erinnerungskultur in Kolumbien und Venezuela.* Munich: C. H. Beck, 2005.

———. "Die Welser in Venezuela—Das Scheitern ihrer wirschaftlichen Ziele." In *Die Welser: Neue Forschungen zur Geschichte und Kultur der oberdeutschen Handelshauses,* edited by Mark Häberlein and Johannes Burkhardt, 285–319. Berlin: Akademie Verlag, 2002.

Federmann, Nikolaus. *Jndianische Historia: EJn schöne kurtzweilge Historia Niclaus Federmanns des Jüngern von Ulm erster raise so er von Hispania und Andolosia ausz in Jndias des Occeanischen Mörs gethan hat / vnd was ihm allda begegnet biß auff sein wiederkunfft inn Hispaniam auffs kurtzest beschriben / gantz lustig zů lesen.* Haguenau: Sigmund Bund, 1557. [HAB A: 180.8 Quod. (4)]

Ferguson, R. Brian, and Neil L. Whitehead. "The Violent Edge of Empire." In *War in the Tribal Zone: Expanding States and Indigenous Warfare,* edited by R. Brian Ferguson and Neil L. Whitehead, 1–30. Santa Fe: School of American Research Press, 2000.

Francis, John Michael. *Invading Colombia: Spanish Accounts of the Gonzalo Jiménez de Quesada Expedition of Conquest.* University Park: Penn State University Press, 2007.

Großhaupt, Walter. "Der Venezuela-Vertrag der Welser." *Scripta mercaturae* 24 (1990): 1–35.

Häberlein, Mark. *The Fuggers of Augsburg: Pursuing Wealth and Honor in Renaissance Germany.* Charlottesville: University of Virginia Press, 2012.

Harbsmeier, Michael. "Gifts and Discoveries: Gift Exchange in Early Modern Narratives of Exploration and Discovery." In *Negotiating the Gift: Pre-Modern Figurations of Exchange,* edited by Gadi Algazi, Valentin Groebner, and Bernhard Jussen, 381–410. Göttingen: Vandenhoeck & Ruprecht, 2003.

———. *Wilde Völkerkunde: Andere Welten in deutschen Reiseberichten der Frühen Neuzeit.* Frankfurt am Main: Campus-Verlag, 1994.

Hassig, Ross. "Aztec and Spanish Conquest in Mesoamerica." In *War in the Tribal Zone: Expanding States and Indigenous Warfare,* edited by Brian R. Ferguson and Neil L. Whitehead, 83–102. Santa Fe: School of American Research Press, 2000.

Hinz, Felix. "Spanish-Indian Encounters. The Conquest and Creation of New Empires." In *The Routledge History of Western Empires,* edited by Robert Aldrich and Kirsten McKenzie, 17–32. London: Routledge, 2014.

Johnson, Christine R. *The German Discovery of the World: Renaissance Encounters with the Strange and Marvelous.* Charlottesville: University of Virginia Press, 2008.

Kellenbenz, Hermann, ed. *Die Fugger in Spanien und Portugal bis 1560: Ein Großunternehmen des 16. Jahrhunderts.* 3 vols. Munich: Ernst Vögel, 1990.

Las Casas, Bartholomé de. *An Account, Much Abbreviated, of the Destruction of the Indies.* Translated by Andrew Hurley. Indianapolis: Hackett, 2003.

Laviña, Javier, and Michael Zeuske. "Failures of Atlantization: First Slaveries in Venezuela and Nueva Granada." *Review (Fernand Braudel Center)* 31, no. 3 (2008): 297–342.

Livi-Bacci, Massimo. *Conquest: The Destruction of the American Indios.* Translated by Carl Ipsen. Cambridge: Polity Press, 2008.

Márquez, Joaquín Gabaldón. *Descubrimiento y conquista de Venezuela: Textos históricos contemporáneos y documentos fundamentales.* 2 vols. Caracas: Academia Nacional de la Historia, 1962.

Mendoza, Rubén G., and Shari R. Harder. "Mythologies of Conquest: Demystifying Amerindian Warfare and European Triumphalism in the Americas." In *The Ethics of Anthropology and Amerindian Research: Reporting on Environmental Degradation and Warfare,* edited by Richard J. Chacon and Rubén G. Mendoza, 191–234. New York: Springer, 2012.

Montenegro, Giovanna. "Conquistadors and Indians 'Fail' at Gift Exchange: An Analysis of Nikolaus Federmann's Indianische Historia (Haguenau, 1557)." *Modern Language Notes* 132, no. 2 (2017): 272–90.

———. "Textual and Visual Representations of the New World: German and Spanish Perspectives of the Conquest of Venezuela in the Sixteenth Century." PhD diss., University of California, Davis, 2013.

Morison, Samuel Eliot. *The European Discovery of America: The Southern Voyages, A.D. 1492–1616*. New York: Oxford University Press, 1974.

Orique, David Thomas. *To Heaven or to Hell: Bartolomé de Las Casas's Confesionario*. University Park: Penn State University Press, 2018.

Pastor Bodmer, Beatriz. *The Armature of Conquest: Spanish Accounts of the Discovery of America, 1492–1589*. Stanford: Stanford University Press, 1992.

Pérez, Berta E. "Rethinking Venezuelan Anthropology." *Ethnohistory* 47, nos. 3–4 (2000): 513–33.

Perri, Michael. "'Ruined and Lost': Spanish Destruction of the Pearl Coast in the Early Sixteenth Century." *Environment and History* 15 (2009): 129–61.

Restall, Matthew. *Seven Myths of the Spanish Conquest*. Oxford: Oxford University Press, 2003.

Ribas, Rosa. *Testimonios de la conciencia lingüística en textos de viajeros alemanes a America en el siglo XVI*. Kassel: Edition Reichenberger, 2005.

Rojas, Roberto Valcárcel, Alice V. M. Samson, and Menno L. P. Hoogland. "Indo-Hispanic Dynamics: From Contact to Colonial Interaction in the Greater Antilles." *International Journal of Historical Archaeology* 17 (2013): 18–39.

Rosas González, Otilia Margarita. "La población indígena en la Provincia de Venezuela." PhD diss., Universidad de Salamanca, 2015.

Roth, Julia. "Sugar and Slaves: The Augsburg Welser as Conquerors of America and Colonial Foundational Myths." *Atlantic Studies* 14, no. 4 (2017): 436–56.

Santana-Quintana, M. Cristina. "Las huellas del español en textos alemanes en la época de la colonización: Nikolaus Federmann (1505–1542)." *RILCE: Revista de Filología Hispánica* 35, no. 2 (2019): 670–87.

Scaramelli, Franz, and Kay Tarble de Scaramelli. "The Roles of Material Culture in the Colonization of the Orinoco, Venezuela." *Journal of Social Archaeology* 5, no. 1 (2005): 135–68.

Seed, Patricia. *Ceremonies of Possession in Europe's Conquest of the New World, 1492–1640*. Cambridge: Cambridge University Press, 1995.

Simmer, Götz. *Gold und Sklaven: Die Provinz Venezuela während der Welser-Verwaltung (1528–1556)*. Berlin: Wissenschaft und Technik, 2000.

Stone, Erin. "War and Rescate: The Sixteenth-Century Circum-Caribbean Indigenous Slave Trade." In *The Spanish Caribbean and the Atlantic World in the Long Sixteenth Century*, edited by Ida Altman and David Wheat, 47–68. Lincoln: University of Nebraska Press, 2019.

Thomas, Hugh. *The Golden Empire: Spain, Charles V, and the Creation of America*. New York: Random House, 2010.

Tyce, Spencer R. "German Conquistadors and Venture Capitalists: The Welser Company's Commercial Experiment in 16th Century Venezuela and the Caribbean World." PhD diss., Ohio State University, 2015.

———. "The Hispano German Caribbean: South German Merchants and the Realities of European Consolidation, 1500–1540." In *The Spanish Caribbean and the Atlantic World in the Long Sixteenth Century*, edited by Ida Altman and David Wheat, 235–56. Lincoln: University of Nebraska Press, 2019.

Vilches, Elvira. "Columbus's Gift: Representations of Grace and Wealth and the Enterprise of the Indies." *Modern Language Notes* 119, no. 2 (2004): 201–25.

Wagner, Sabine. "Nikolaus Federmanns Jndianische Historia: Zum Verhältnis von offizieller Reiseberichterstattung und juristischer Rhetorik." *Frühneuzeit-Info* 5, no. 2 (1994): 164–72.

Warsh, Molly A. *American Baroque: Pearls and the Nature of Empire, 1492–1700*. Chapel Hill: University of North Carolina Press, 2018.

Wojciehowski, Hannah Chapelle. *Group Identity in the Renaissance World*. Cambridge: Cambridge University Press, 2011.

Items marked with an *asterisk denote a place name mentioned by Federmann for which there is no known location and modern equivalent.

Acarigua, 8, 15, 69–70, 72–75, 88–89
Acarigua River, 70n123
Achagua, 52–57, 59, 61, 102
Algarve, 105
alliances
    between Indigenous nations, 43, 45, 47, 50, 93–95, 102
    with Indigenous nations, 20–21, 42, 50, 54, 70–71
Ampiés, Juan. See Martínez de Ampiés, Juan
Andalusia, 23–24
anthropophagy, 18, 38, 52, 56, 56n111, 59
Arabs, 25–28
Aroa, Sierra de, 99n171
Aruba, 31n77, 32n79
arquebus, 19, 40, 40n97, 85n155
arrows, poisoned, 4, 52, 65, 70, 84, 93
asiento, 1, 3–4, 16, 21
Aticares, 102
Atlantic Ocean, 23, 24, 28, 89n159, 101n174
Audiencia Real. See Real Audiencia
Augsburg 1, 5, 8, 13, 71n128, 107
Ayamanes, 5, 19, 38–50, 55, 56, 102
Ayamonte, 106
Azores, 105
Azua de Compostela, 34, 34n84

baptism. See conversion
Bararida. See Vararida
Barquisimeto, 8, 14, 15, 57–59, 59n116, 61, 66, 69, 89–92, 99, 103

Belalcázar, Sebastián de, 9
Berbery, 25
Bogotá, 4, 9
Bonaire, 30, 31n77, 32n79
Bry, Theodor de, 10
buckler. See shield
Bund, Sigmund, 10, 107

Cabo de la Vela, 4
Cabo de Maracapana, 4
Cabot (Caboto), John, 76n136
Cabot (Caboto), Sebastian, 76, 76n136, 81
*Cacaridi, 54
Cádiz, 106
Canary Islands, 24, 28
cannibalism. See anthropophagy
Cape St. Vincent (Cabo de São Vicente), 105
Caquetíos, 14, 16, 18, 32n79, 37, 55, 56–62, 70, 73, 74, 78–80, 82, 86, 87, 90–96, 97, 100–103
Caracas, 3
*Carahao, 84–86
Caribbean Current, 30–31, 30n79
Caribbean Sea, 8, 101n173–74
*Carohana, 47, 47n106
Carora, 47n106
Cartagena, 9
Carvajal, Juan de, 4
Casa de Contratación, 5
Castile, 106
*Cathary, 88
Catholic Church, 17, 21
*Cazaradadi, 76–77
Charles I, king of Spain. See Charles V of Habsburg
Charles V of Habsburg, 3, 9, 11, 16
chickens, 80, 80n147

Churuguara, 38n95
Ciparicotos, 59, 91, 96–102
clergy, Catholic, 12, 42n102, 98, 98n168
*Coaheri River, 62, 62n118, 77, 80, 82, 84
*Coary, 54
Colón, Hernando, 71, 71n126
Colombia, 4
Columbus (Colón), Christopher, 2, 7, 11,
    18, 19, 71n126, 71n127
Cojedes River (Coaheri), 59n 116, 62,
    62n118, 75n134, 77, 80, 81n151,
    82, 84
communication problems, 18, 55, 66, 100
contract. See *asiento*
conversion, 17, 42, 42n102–3, 43, 46
Cordillera Oriental, 8, 9
Coro, 3, 4, 7–9, 12, 15, 18, 24, 29–37,
    32n81, 34n83, 46, 48, 54–57, 59,
    80–81, 88, 89, 93, 99–103
Cortés, Hernán, 7, 11, 71, 71n124, 71n127
cougar, 78n144
Council of the Indies, 9, 11
Coyones, 70, 73–77, 88
crossbow, 19, 65, 65n120, 70, 84, 104
Cuibas, 59, 61–73, 89, 99, 102
Cumaná, 2, 4
Cundinamarca, 9, 13
Curaçao, 30, 32n79
*Curahamara, 77, 78–80, 83, 85, 87–88,
    94
*Curahy, 76

Dalfinger, Ambrosius, 2, 4, 7–8, 12,
    20n53, 21, 24, 35–36, 35n86,
    102n179
Danube, 80, 80n145
Dávila, Pedro Arias, 7, 71, 71n125,
    71n127
demonization
    of Europeans, 48, 48n108, 52, 53
    of Indigenous people, 42, 77, 90
Díaz de Solís, Juan, 76n137
disease
    among Europeans, 8, 36, 60–61, 64,
        69–71, 79, 89, 102–3
    among Indigenous people, 29, 43
    concealing illness and death, 21, 51,
        60, 84
    introduced by Europeans, 5, 19, 29n70,
        36, 43, 43n104
    See also fever and smallpox

dogs, 19, 64, 97, 97n166
ducat (ducado), 27, 27n67, 106
dwarfs, 38, 42–49, 42n101

Ecuador, 4
Ehinger, Georg, 2, 3, 33
Ehinger, Heinrich, 3
Ehinger, Ulrich, 3, 7, 24
El Baúl, 75n133, 82n152
El Dorado, 9, 19
encomienda, 29n69
enemies, Europeans outnumbered by, 20,
    56–57, 59, 64, 70, 71–72, 83–84,
    91–93
enslavement
    by Arabs, 26n66
    by Indigenous nations, 81, 81n149,
        89–90
    by Spanish piracy in the Caribbean,
        31–33, 32n79, 100–1, 106
    gift of humans, 18, 48, 58, 74–75, 81,
        88, 89
    of Africans, 2
    of Indigenous people by Europeans,
        2–3, 3n10, 8, 18, 29, 29n69, 32,
        32n79, 42, 74, 81, 88, 89
entrada, 1, 4–5, 7–9, 11–13, 17–18, 35–36,
    35n86, 35n89

factor, 3, 30, 32n80, 35
Faro, 106
fever, recurring, 8, 36, 69, 88, 88n158,
    93, 103
fire as weapon against Indigenous people,
    17, 19, 42, 67–68, 73, 74, 84, 94–95
food
    difficulty securing supplies, 53, 62,
        78–79, 85
    lack of, 62–63, 69, 96–99, 105–6
    not fit to eat, 63, 69, 98
    provided by Indigenous nations, 33, 40,
        47, 54, 57, 64, 67, 70, 78–79
    See also hunt
Fugger Company, 1–2

Galeras del Baúl, 82n152
Gayones, 49–53, 55–56
Ghent, 9
gemstones, 23, 60
gifts, 17, 18, 23
    exchange, 58, 100

forestalled, 48, 93
given to caciques, 41–42, 47, 51, 53–54, 57, 65, 77, 89–90, 92, 100
given to Indigenous people, 39, 49, 67, 69
of humans. *See* enslavement
received from Indigenous people, non-submissive, 18, 59
received from Indigenous people, submissive, 37, 48, 49, 50, 52, 54, 58, 69, 70, 76, 90, 101, 102
value of, 18, 39, 54, 58, 67, 68, 69
gold
gifted by Federmann, 43
greed for, 18, 58, 60, 67–68, 95, 106
naturally occurring, 29, 37, 56, 60
received from Indigenous people, 23, 37–38, 48–49, 52, 54, 56, 58, 62, 67–68, 70, 90, 100
Gottfried. Johann Ludwig, 10
Guaiqueríes, 75, 77–90, 102
guilder, Rhenish, 58n114

Haguenau, 10, 107
*Hamadoa, 80–81
Herrera, Sancho de, 28, 28n68
Hispaniola, 2–5, 29, 29n70, 30n73, 32n79, 103n180
Hitotos, 91, 101
*Hittova, 38–39, 38n95,
Hohermuth von Speyer, Georg, 4, 9
horses, 7, 30
advantage in battle, 19, 20, 57, 64, 68, 71–72, 86
Indigenous fear of, 19, 39, 57, 68. 71
useless in difficult terrain, 8, 38, 45–46, 52, 55, 64, 75, 81–82, 89
Hulsius, Levinus, 10
hunger. *See* food, lack of
hunt, 64, 66, 98–99
Hutten, Philipp von, 4

illness. *See* disease
immortality of Europeans, Indigenous belief in, 21, 51, 51n109, 60
incursion. See *entrada*
Inquisition, Spanish, 10
interpreters. Indigenous, 18, 32, 37, 39, 46, 50, 53, 55, 57–58, 67
*Itabana, 75–76, 75n133, 78–85, 88, 102–3

jaguar, 78n144, 96, 98–99
Jiménez de Quesada, Gonzalo, 9
Jirajaras, 14, 16, 37–39, 43, 45, 55, 56, 102–3

Kiffhaber, Hans, 10–13, 23–24

La Gomera, 16, 28
languages, Indigenous, 16, 17, 29, 55, 62, 66, 82, 91, 100
See also communication problems and interpreters, Indigenous
Lanzarote, 16, 24, 25, 27, 28n68
Las Casas, Bartolomé de, 2, 20
Laubenberg, Johann Wilhelm von, 23
Lerma, García de, 3, 3n12
López de Palacios Rubios, Juan, 12
Lutheran, 10, 42n103

Magdalena River Valley, 4, 9
malaria. *See* fever, recurring
Manaure, 100, 100n172
Maracaibo Lake, 4, 35n86
Martínez de Ampiés, Juan, 3, 32, 32n81, 100n172
*Martinico, 101, 103
Medina del Campo, 106
mile, Spanish, 7, 16, 24n62
mining, miners, 1, 3, 4, 7, 21, 24, 29, 32n79, 37
Miraca, 15
Mona Island, 103, 103n180
Moors, 106

Narváez, Pánfilo de, 7
Naveros, Antonio de, 8, 11–12, 24n60, 101n177
Nicaragua, 71, 71n125
notary, 8, 11, 12, 101, 101n177

officials, Spanish, 4, 12, 13, 21, 23–24, 35, 101, 101n177
Ojeda, Alonso de, 2
Orinoco River Basin, 4–5, 8, 15, 17, 18

Pacific Ocean, 3, 8, 19, 37, 37n91, 46, 59–60, 69, 73–76, 80, 102
Padrón Real, 5
Panamá, 71n125
Paraguaná Peninsula, 31n76–77, 33, 34
Paraná River, 76n138

Pearl Coast, 2
pearls, 2, 60, 106
peso, 58, 58n113
Pinzón, Vicente Yáñez, 2
piracy, Spanish. *See* enslavement
Plata, Río de la, 76, 76n136–38
Portugal, 2, 28, 105
Portuguesa River, 88n157
presents. *See* gifts
probanza de mérito, 11, 16, 71–72,
    72n129, 102
    See also report
Puerto Rico, 34n85, 103n180

Real Audiencia, 7, 9, 29
relación. *See* report
Rentz, Sebastian, 30, 30n72, 34, 103, 106
report, 4, 5, 8, 10–13, 16, 21, 71–72,
    71n128, 72n129, 93, 102
requerimiento, 16–17, 38n94, 42n99,
    42n103, 48
Rhine River, 101
Ribeiro, Diogo, 5–7

Sailer, Hieronymus, 3
San Germán, 34
San Juan, 34, 34n85
Sanlúcar de Barrameda, 5, 7, 16, 24, 34
Santa Ana de Coro. *See* Coro
Saona Island, 34
Saragossa, 2
Sarmiento, Luis, 33, 33n82, 35, 35n88
Santo Domingo, 2, 3, 7–9, 16, 28–36, 71,
    71n127, 100–3
Santa Marta, 3–4, 9
Seissenhofer, Hans, 35–36, 35n87
Seitz, Hieronymus, 71, 71n128
Seville, 2, 3, 5, 8, 24n61, 35, 76n136,
    105–6
shield, 44, 87, 95
slaves. *See* enslavement
smallpox, 5, 19, 29, 29n71, 43

Solis, Río de, 76, 76n137
South Sea. *See* Pacific Ocean
Spain, 3, 9, 23–25, 34, 35,103, 105–6
    See also Andalusia and Castile
Spanish Crown, 1, 3, 11, 13, 21
sword, 19, 20, 64, 83, 86, 94, 95

*Temeri River, 88, 88n157
Terceira, 105
Tierra Firme, 2, 30n75
Tocuyo River, 38n95, 44
*Tohibara, 75–76
torture, 14, 17, 77, 85, 87, 97
Turbio River, 59n116

Ulm, 5, 10, 23–24, 30, 35, 80n145, 106

Valencia, 2
Valladolid, 8, 10
Valle de las Damas, 92
Vanicero, Cara, 37
Vararida, 59, 59n116, 92, 103
Vázquez de Acuña, Alonso, 11
Vázquez de Ayllón, Lucas, 7

waterspout, 103–5, 104n182
weapons, 19
    European. *See* arquebus, crossbow, fire,
        shield, and sword
    Indigenous, 19, 76, 95 (*see also* arrows,
        poisonous)
Welser Company, 1–9, 12–13, 20–21, 24,
    30, 32n81, 34, 35, 35n87, 103
Welser, Bartholomäus V, 9, 24
Welser, Bartholomäus VI, 4

*Xaragua, 101, 103

Yaracuy River, 8, 101
Yucatán, 71, 71n124

Zarco, Bartolomé, 101, 101n176

latin american originals

Series Editor | Matthew Restall

This series features primary source texts on colonial and nineteenth-century Latin America, translated into English, in slim, accessible, affordable editions that also make scholarly contributions. Most of these sources are published here in English for the first time and represent an alternative to the traditional texts on early Latin America. The initial focus of the series was on the conquest period in sixteenth-century Spanish America, but its scope now includes later centuries and aims to be hemispheric. LAO volumes feature archival documents and printed sources originally in Spanish, Portuguese, Italian, Latin, Nahuatl, Maya and other Native American languages. The contributing authors are historians, anthropologists, art historians, geographers, and scholars of literature.

Matthew Restall is Edwin Erle Sparks Professor of Latin American History and Anthropology, and Director of Latin American Studies, at the Pennsylvania State University. He edited *Ethnohistory* for a decade and now co-edits the *Hispanic American Historical Review*.

Titles in Print

Invading Colombia: Spanish Accounts of the Gonzalo Jiménez de Quesada Expedition of Conquest (LAO 1)
J. Michael Francis

Invading Guatemala: Spanish, Nahua, and Maya Accounts of the Conquest Wars (LAO 2)
Matthew Restall and Florine G. L. Asselbergs

The Conquest on Trial: Carvajal's "Complaint of the Indians in the Court of Death" (LAO 3)
Carlos A. Jáuregui

Defending the Conquest: Bernardo de Vargas Machuca's "Defense and Discourse of the Western Conquests" (LAO 4)
Edited by Kris Lane and translated by Timothy F. Johnson

Forgotten Franciscans: Works from an Inquisitional Theorist, a Heretic, and an Inquisitional Deputy (LAO 5)
Martin Austin Nesvig

Gods of the Andes: An Early Jesuit Account of Inca Religion and Andean Christianity (LAO 6)
Sabine Hyland

Of Cannibals and Kings: Primal Anthropology in the Americas (LAO 7)
Neil L. Whitehead

Translated Christianities: Nahuatl and Maya Religious Texts (LAO 8)
Mark Z. Christensen

The Improbable Conquest: Sixteenth-Century Letters from the Río de la Plata (LAO 9)
Pablo García Loaeza and Victoria L. Garrett

The Native Conquistador: Alva Ixtlilxochitl's Account of the Conquest of New Spain (LAO 10)
Edited and translated by Amber Brian, Bradley Benton, and Pablo García Loaeza

The History of the New World: Benzoni's "Historia del Mondo Nuovo" (LAO 11)
Translated by Jana Byars and edited by Robert C. Schwaller and Jana Byars

Contesting Conquest: Indigenous Perspectives on the Spanish Occupation of Nueva Galicia (LAO 12)
Ida Altman

To Heaven or to Hell: Bartolomé de Las Casas's "Confesionario" (LAO 13)
David Thomas Orique, O.P.

To the Shores of Chile: The "Journal and History" of the Brouwer Expedition to Valdivia in 1643 (LAO 14)
Mark Meuwese

Baptism Through Incision: The Postmortem Cesarean Operation in the Spanish Empire (LAO 15)
Martha Few, Zeb Tortorici, and Adam Warren, translated by Nina M. Scott

Indigenous Life After the Conquest: The De la Cruz Family Papers of Colonial Mexico (LAO 16)
Caterina Pizzigoni and Camilla Townsend

An Irish Rebel in New Spain (LAO 17)
Andrea Martínez Baracs

Pandemic in Potosí: Fear, Loathing, and Public Piety in a Colonial Mining Metropolis (LAO 18)
Kris Lane